Winning the Australian Real Estate Game: How to Earn Your First Million Through Property Investing and Finally Quit Your 9-5

Digital Version ISBN: 978-0-6456269-0-2

Paper Back ISBN: 978-0-6456269-1-9

AF797599

Dedication

I would like to dedicate this book to the many important people in my life.

First of all, I am grateful for my parents and siblings. They have imparted many valuable lessons on the importance of love, discipline and hard work. The time we spent together as a family showed me what it meant to help each other grow and to surround yourself with good people.

This book would also not have been possible without the encouragement of my beautiful wife, Illa Gupta, and our little daughter, Amaya. Their constant support was vital throughout the course of my property investment journey. It was because of them that I continued the work that changed our lives for the better.

I would also like to thank all of my mentors, especially Dymphna Boholt. She taught me the value of setting goals and taking massive action in the world of property.

And lastly, I want to give a special mention to all the leaders and investors who I've met along the way. You have, in many ways, inspired me to believe in myself and to trust the process.

Success Stories: https://investorsdream.com.au/testimonials/

"Investors Dream made things simple for us. Being first-time investors, we felt overwhelmed about what to do and how to do things. Sanjeev set us up with an educational program where we learned a lot about what we actually wanted, which we had not thought about prior. My experience was above and beyond what I thought I would get."- **Nadene**

Nadene and Paul are a young couple with two kids. They are busy professionals based in Sydney where they own a plumbing business and work as an educator in the logistics industry. Being time-poor and first-time investors, they were looking for a trusted buyer's agent to guide them and ensure great outcomes on their investment

—

"Sanjeev educated us the right way so that, moving forward, if we plan to do investment, of course, it is going to benefit us. So looking forward to working again with Investors Dream." - **Prasad and Pratibha**

Prasad and Pratibha wanted to invest in properties and were looking for a buyer's agent. They were sceptical at first. But according to them, Sanjeev of Investors Dream made things seamless and guided them right throughout the process. He started with education to make sure that they understand the processes involved. From unsure to 100% sure, Prasad and Pratibha were so happy with their investment property purchase.

—

"It was 100% worth the investment. I'm already looking for my next property purchase with them and future investments to come." - **Marissa**

Marissa was looking to buy an investment property for a long time, but she didn't know where to start. So, she reached out to Investors Dream. She found that Sanjeev is trustworthy and the process was seamless.

Sanjeev didn't just help Marissa to find a property but he also provided education so that she will know all the property investment processes. She added that the services provided by Sanjeev and his team are worth it. And she's already looking for her next property with the help and guidance of Investors Dream.

—

"The only regret I had was I hadn't known about Investors Dream earlier. Because with Sanjeev as a buyer's agent, I am not just a number. Investors Dream seriously help their clients not just to purchase a property but to educate them about investment strategies and the property market as well." - **Joel**

Joel was looking for a buyers agent where the client is not just a number but they are serious about helping their clients. He was in touch with other buyer's agents before but still decided to go with Investors Dream for his third investment purchase. And soon after, he signed for his fourth purchase.

According to Joel, the whole process of working with Sanjeev was fantastic. He was very professional from start to finish. Sanjeev provided a rigorous education process with proven results through case studies and success stories.

—

"It's all worth it working with Sanjeev of Investors Dream. His strategies and case studies helped make my investment property journey a success." - **Nowshad**

Nowshad knew some property agents before, but he said that he was not that comfortable with the strategies they were presenting as they lacked data. But Sanjeev supported everything with his case studies. And that gave him the confidence to use the services of Investors Dream.

Nowshad added that Sanjeev was not into just buying a property but also made sure that he was updated with all that was happening. His knowledge, professionalism, transparency and strategies made the whole process seamless. He also mentioned that he was satisfied with the service provided by Investors Dream, which is why he is looking for his next investment property with Sanjeev and his team.

Google Reviews: https://investorsdream.com.au/reviews/

Sunil Gupta

When we decided to purchase an investment property, we thought of having professional help from a buyer's agent who is knowledgeable and trustworthy.

We chose Investors Dream because we have seen the professionalism of the whole team from start to finish. Sanjeev is very knowledgeable in the Australian property market. We were amazed at how he handles his clients by providing education so that we could understand the whole process and help us narrow down our options based on our set goals.

Through the help of Investors Dream, we were able to purchase a great positive cashflow property in a high capital growth area. Before we thought that building a property portfolio was hard but after working with Sanjeev and his team, we realised that it's not that hard because we were educated well and at the same time the journey was seamless.

In fact, we recently signed up for another property. Highly recommended to anyone who wants to start their investment property or build their property portfolio.

John Rusell

8 years ago, I purchased my first investment property through a very popular (and expensive) buyer's agent. But it turned out to be a very wrong investment. I had to sell that property and I am lucky that I discovered Sanjeev through a friend of mine.

I loved his personalised approach. He guided us based on our personal circumstances and long-term goals. He found the right property for us and, as a result, in the last 12 months, we purchased 3 more properties with him. He is knowledgeable with a deep understanding of the various markets, and he is very good at coming up with a strategy that suits your current needs and long-term goals.

We faced a few issues during this journey but Sanjeev was very patient with us. He answered all the questions and guided us in the right direction. That took away all the anxiety. Now, all our properties are positive cash flow and all of them have grown by 5-10% in just 1 year.

I would not hesitate even a bit to recommend his services to anyone. It will be your best decision to work with him.

Phuong Vu

I'm aiming for property investing long term, then I found out what Sanjeev has been able to achieve through property investing. It is the exact path that I want—to become a full-time property investor with less risk. Sanjeev has shown me that he's not here just to do a hard sale but to help and guide me through my whole property investment journey.

I chose Investors Dream because Sanjeev is genuine and his ultimate goal is to see me learn, grow and achieve all my property deals and goals. As a buyer's agent, Sanjeev has always acted in my best interest and his communication skill is just superb. He guided me through every single step of the way and he's always there to support and guide me. I'm comfortable working with him, even though we don't know each other for a long time.

What Sanjeev has to offer is far beyond being a buyer's agent. With his service, he didn't just save me time, which is money. Sanjeev guided me through all the strategies and showed me how to achieve each goal with the fewest risks possible. It's worth the investment.

I can't wait to finish off my first deal with a big win so I can quickly move on to the next one. I will definitely recommend Sanjeev and Investors Dream to my friends, family or anyone looking for property investment services.

Hari Krishna Manchana

Sanjeev is a very trustworthy person. His hard work reflects on his success stories. Being a seasoned investor myself, there are areas with some risks of which even I am not aware. And going with Investors Dream helped me to take the edge off those risks. Investors Dream's processes, education and communication were very helpful in securing a good investment property. Sanjeev with his extensive knowledge and resources helped us to secure an off-market property for around 10% less than the market value.

I was very impressed with his market knowledge, process and his determination to help people grow their wealth through property. I am looking to buy another investment property through Investors Dream. I would highly recommend them to family and friends to grow their property investment portfolio or to someone looking to buy their first investment property.

Kevin D'Souza

We were looking for our next investment property with some creative strategies to purchase a high cashflow property, and for a professional team whom we can trust and seek timely support & guidance.

I came across Sanjeev's profile on LinkedIn and got in touch with him. We found Sanjeev is very knowledgeable and walks the talk. He is passionate about property and we felt we could trust him. The communication was open and straightforward; Sanjeev made us very comfortable by answering all our queries and helped us to narrow down our decision by giving the right strategies and explaining the pros & cons. He even recommended a mortgage broker and conveyancer and found an excellent managing agent.

Finally, Investors Dream secured a property for us before the auction, which we bought for at least $50,000 below market value. The property has a positive cash flow of $13,000 per annum. We are extremely happy working with Investors Dream and are already recommending them to our family & friends. In fact, I would recommend them to anyone who is looking for a quality service in purchasing an ideal and strategic investment property with ease.

We are already discussing our second purchase with Investors Dream. Thank you Sanjeev & the team at Investors Dream for all your hard work and amazing service.

Kurt Castell-Brown

I chose Investors Dream as I was looking to purchase my investment property but also wanted to learn about various property strategies, pros and cons, risks involved, overall process and much more, which was very crucial for me before buying any property.

I really loved and enjoyed working with Investors Dream as they made my first investment property journey seamless and provided me with enough education at each stage of purchasing. Sanjeev and the entire team are very professional. Sanjeev was always available to answer any questions I had along the way and kept me updated throughout the process.

Finally, we purchased a property off-the-market for $372K, which we immediately rented out for $430 a week ($20 more than what was initially suggested) which gives me around $7K positive cashflow a year. The property also has the potential for a granny flat, which can further boost the cash flow to $13K annually. I would highly recommend Sanjeev and Investors Dream to anyone looking for help and mitigating any risk while purchasing their first investment property or building a property portfolio.

Dan Strazdins

I chose Investors Dream because I was looking for a property that I could initially live in and would turn into an investment property. Investors Dream was recommended to me by my family. My parents used Investors Dream to purchase one of their investment properties and Sanjeev came highly recommended.

Working with Investors Dream was really easy. It involved processes and Sanjeev really helped me understand or narrow down what I was looking for, what I was after and the best way to go about that.

There was really an involvement in the process and I feel like I was kept in the loop along the way, which was really great.

Using Investors Dream was a worthwhile investment for me. Sanjeev was able to give me some great insights into looking for different types of properties and looking in areas that I haven't thought of looking at. He also educated me as an investor on what I should be looking for in a property to make sure that I get the best deal and the best investment.

I will definitely recommend Investors Dream to my family and friends who are looking at purchasing an investment property. I really like the flexibility of working with Sanjeev and Investors Dream because I'm not a traditional investor. I want a property that I could live in first as well and so that was a really good experience for me.

Tim Edmondson

Well what an IP journey Sanjeev has guided us through! He skilfully navigated our location and price matrix to clarify an area with growth markers, negotiated a great house that settled during the March '20 lockdown, and then continued great service and advice to have it tenanted within 3 weeks of settlement. Value is up 20% in that 12 months.

I highly recommend Sanjeev's buyer's agent service. I have already referred him to family members and he just helped us find our son's first home (at a good discount to value!). Thanks, Sanjeev!

Winning the Australian Real Estate Game

How to Earn Your First Million Through Property Investing and Finally Quit Your 9-5

Sanjeev Sah

Table of Contents

Foreword 1

Real Estate Success Journeys May Be Different but the Nuts and Bolts Never Change 5

- Capital Growth of $85,000 in Six Months..... 9
- Cash Flow of $8,632 in Two Years 10
- A 23-Year Old Landscaper With a Capital Growth of $67,000 in Seven Months 12
- Real Estate Isn't About Your Background – It's About Making the Right Moves 14

From Zero-Knowledge to a Multi-Million Dollar Portfolio in Five Years (Who Am I and Why Should You Listen to Me?) 16

- Establishing a Thriving Career Out of College 18
- Rekindling an Old Flame..... 19
- Making One Careful Investing Decision After Another..... 20
- Transitioning Out of Corporate 21
- Finally Taking the Leap Towards Full-Time Property Investing..... 22
- The Common Ground Across All My Deals 26
- Paying it Forward 27

The Different Stages of Your Property Investment Journey 29

- The Stages of Your Property Journey..... 29

The Property Quartet 36

- Focusing on Positive Cash Flow Properties 37
- Investing for Capital Growth..... 39
- Using Value Add Strategies 40
- Buying Under Value..... 41

Cash Flow Is the Lifeblood of Your Business..... 43

- Real Estate Investment Is About Improving Cash Flow..... 45

Positive Cash Flow Improves Serviceability 50
It's a Buffer Against Interest Rate Rises 55
Generate Your Own Capital Growth 59
Supply and Demand 59
Population, Infrastructure, Employment – The Capital Growth Drivers to Look For 64
Employment 68
Achieving True Wealth 70
The Short Term Is Always Tougher 73
Four Value-Add Strategies to Supercharge Your Portfolio 77
Granny Flat 80
Renovation 83
Subdivision 87
New Build 91
Buying Under Value to Accelerate Your Wealth 95
Buying Below Replacement Cost 96
What Incentivises Sellers to Sell Quickly 100
Familiarising Yourself With an Area 104
Property Financing Fundamentals 108
Know Your Options for Potential Lenders 108
Know How Mortgages Work 110
Understanding Equity 112
Crunch Your Numbers 115
Learn to Negotiate Loans 116
Investment Structures 118
Factors to Consider Before Choosing an Investment Structure 120
What Investment Structures Are Available for You? 122

Choosing the Right Investment Structure 127
The Property Investor Mindset 129
Have a Long-Term Vision 132
The Importance of Setting Goals and Knowing Your WHY 135
Why You Need to Set Property Investment Goals 137
How to Set Your Goals 139
Looking into Your Future Property Investment Journey 144

Foreword

I first got the idea of writing this book after my mentor, Ben Handler, mentioned it to me in early 2022. He told me that my wife and I have a very inspirational story and sharing it would inspire and bring value to more people who are looking to start their property investment journey.

You see, my wife and I had set a goal for me to become a full-time investor back in 2015. We wanted to build a good property portfolio, quit our 9-5 jobs, and live our lives on our own terms.

This all came true in less than 5 years.

And throughout that time, we have also been helping hundreds of Australians build their property portfolio after starting our company, Investors Dream Pty Ltd.

But before I became a full-time career property investor, my life was pretty different.

I was living in India, completing my Engineering degree in Computer Science. Soon after, I got into the IT industry.

At age 30, I heard the term 'passive income' for the very first time. Unfortunately, this concept was never taught to us at school or university, even though I went to reputable institutions.

So, as soon as I understood the meaning and importance of the term, I started reading self-development books and looked for people who have achieved great success through passive income.

It was during this period that I also began asking myself why some people have all the money, time, nice cars, and houses. It seemed like everyone was accomplishing this…

…Except me.

Because of this, I wanted to know who these people are and what they did to reach their goals. And after much research, I came to an important realisation:

These people are no different from anyone; they are just regular people.

The only difference was that they were investing in self-education. They set clear goals for themselves and they keep a strong WHY. Also, they have a mission for their life and have found their vehicle for making it happen.

So, I took the cue from these people and started writing my own goals with my wife. Since then, we never looked back.

We decided to take massive action in our property journey and it changed our lives completely. It took me the next 5 years to find a vehicle that could eventually give me a passive income and help build wealth for me and my family.

We understood that what we were doing is only what the minority of the population does.

That's why we surrounded ourselves with like-minded people who were in the same boat. We inspired each other to take more action, rather than settling down for less and living a life with regret.

Along the way, we faced many challenges. Some of them included juggling our 9-5 jobs with investing, family commitments, and allocating time for side hustles.

I remember a day when our daughter was little over a year old.

You see, I used to drop her at the childcare centre in the mornings before going to work. But that day, she was crying and didn't want to go to the childcare centre. She wanted to stay at home because she was feeling a little down.

Still, I had to drop her off at the childcare centre – but only because I couldn't take a day off or work from home.

After dropping her off, I cried on the way to my office. I called my wife saying that I didn't want to live my life like this anymore. I didn't want to sacrifice my time away from my daughter so I could take care of her when she needs me most.

My wife simply said, *"Why are you crying? If you're not happy about it, go change it. What is stopping you from changing your life? Other people are fine with leaving their kids like that. You choose!"*

For a minute, her response shocked me. But I quickly realised that she was right. What was the point of me crying when I was fully capable of doing something about it?

That day, I decided from deep down in my heart that I was going to do whatever it takes to change my and my family's life. My wife and my daughter were my biggest reasons for taking action and realising my property investment goals.

My family was my WHY.

Spending enough time with my daughter was non-negotiable for me. Plus, I wanted to spend enough time with my parents back in India as they were getting older. These thoughts always kept me moving forward.

We understood that building our life and enjoying it on a daily basis was more important than building a career. And to do this, we needed a vehicle that could support our goals.

We found that property investing was the solution for us as it is a proven and tested passive income vehicle for many successful people around the globe.

Since 2015, we have invested hundreds of thousands in our self-education. We made a lot of mistakes on the way, but we also achieved great results for ourselves.

Along the way, a lot of investors started approaching me, asking for help and guidance in their own property investment journey. They were inspired by the success I was able to achieve with my family.

So, in 2019, we started our buyer's agency.

We wanted to help Australians buy investment properties and build their property portfolio. Most importantly, we wanted to help them to not repeat the same mistakes we made when we were starting out.

I also began sharing my insights and experience on property through many channels, most recently on my podcast "Property Uncovered." Here, I interview your average everyday Australian investor so they can share their property journey to inspire others.

This book is a culmination of everything I have learned, discovered, and applied in my own work as a property investor. Through each chapter, I encourage you to join me in taking massive action.

It's time to take the steps to build the life you've always wanted.

CHAPTER 1

Real Estate Success Journeys May Be Different but the Nuts and Bolts Never Change

Abhiram and Pavitra had big dreams.

They wanted to reconnect with their roots and spend some time together in their Indian hometown.

The problem was that they were both working in the IT industry. That meant they couldn't just up and leave Sydney—at least not without a significant source of passive income.

That is why they wanted to buy several investment properties.

They started with one, hoping it would kick off their breakthrough in property investing, but their enthusiasm was soon quelled.

See, the property didn't appreciate in value. Even though it wasn't a negative cash flow unit in Sydney, it hadn't had capital growth in three years.

This wasn't nearly enough to help them accomplish their goals.

So, they tried again.

They purchased a house in regional NSW. It was a 499 square-metre lot that they bought for $340,000.

This time, they didn't leave anything to chance. Knowing that the property wasn't in a very good condition to generate income from the get-go, Abhiram and Pavitra decided to renovate.

Fortunately, the cost of the renovations rang up to just $31,000, putting their total investment at $371,000.

The couple had some doubts whether the purchase and renovation work would pay off, but their concerns proved unfounded.

The property started generating $5,564 in cash flow per year, and the manufactured equity uplift through renovations was a fantastic $39,000.

After two years, the property's value grew by $139,000, meaning it's now worth more than $500,000.

Better yet, Abhiram and Pavitra learned fundamental strategies they could leverage, including high capital growth, a low vacancy rate, positive cash flow, and cosmetic renovations.

They relied on similar methods when they purchased their second property.

It was a house in regional QLD bought for $338,000.

The couple purchased the property for $22,000 under market value, as the owner needed a quick sale. The location was also great – a 993 square metre lot near the beach.

Best of all, this one required no renovations. This allowed the couple to make tremendous cash flow from the start ($5,980 per year).

The two properties were the breakthrough Abhiram and Pavitra had been looking for. With sound investment strategies, they achieved high capital growth of $288,000 and cash flow of nearly $12,000 in just two years.

After these two successful purchases, which changed their mindset and boosted their confidence about investing, they then went ahead and bought two more similar investment properties, the third one in regional and the fourth one in metro.

All these have set them right on the path towards their goal of building another income stream, wealth and living anywhere they want, starting with India.

Real Estate: A Powerful Wealth Generator for Anyone

What Abhiram and Pavitra's story tells is that real estate can be a powerful wealth generator for anyone, as long as you're willing to fine-tune and modify your tactics.

See, many people think that only a select group of people can be successful in property investing. However, that's not the case. You might end up making mistakes like Abriham and Pavitra did in the beginning of their real estate journey, but that doesn't mean you won't be successful.

Especially when you're committed to your goals, willing to learn and take action.

Property prices have exceeded all expectations, reaching a staggering $9.9 trillion at the time of writing this book. This makes the real estate market four times larger than Australia's GDP. It's also more valuable than the GDP of any other country except for China and the U.S.

The Australian property market is red-hot, but what's driving the nearly unprecedented rise in value?

Prior to COVID-19, we already had a housing shortage, but post COVID the situation became worse. Experts believed the coronavirus pandemic would cripple the market, but their predictions were incorrect. Property prices kept rising, and it seems they won't slow down any time soon.

But what does this mean for real estate investors? It means they can expand their portfolio quicker than ever and reap the rewards for being part of this game.

During COVID-19, low-interest rates promoted a real estate boom. Economists expected a crash, but the figures proved them wrong.

In November 2021, Sydney's real estate value increased by 0.9%, which is 25.8% more than 2020. A similar trend was observed in Melbourne, where property prices jumped 0.6% – a 16% rise from 2020. National levels also look fantastic, soaring by 22% in just 12 months.

This is excellent news for people who've kept their jobs. They managed to save money and are now more willing to spend their funds on renovations or purchases. It means realtors are highly confident about the market.

And it was not just the interest rates generating the enthusiasm – household balance sheets have played a pivotal role, too.

There's been a tremendous rise in deposits and saving rates. COVID restrictions limited spending opportunities, but they're finally opening up. As a result, households are analysing the market, and are determining how to spend their money.

The economic landscape is favourable, and it's made many Australian millionaires.

On the list of the 200 richest persons in the country, as many as 63 individuals made their wealth through property investment.

Harry Triguboff, an apartment mogul, defied the economic slowdown in 2020 and grew his wealth by nearly $1 billion.

Hui Wing Mau, another realtor, developed a formidable portfolio estimated at around $9 billion.

But does this mean Triguboff, Mau, and other prosperous investors used the same strategies as previous decades? The answer is no.

Just like Abhiram and Pavitra, they've had to adjust to new conditions, where financing became harder, investment and offshore buying evaporated, and prices fell.

Even Paul Little, the founder of Little Projects, had to adjust his approach, anticipating correctly that offshore buyers and domestic investors would be restricted.

Little moved from high-rise markets and switched to less valuable areas, like student accommodation and hotels. He came out of the restrictions virtually unscathed, with over 200 apartments in Melbourne in his portfolio.

Many other rich listers invested in properties confidently. They traded, expanded, and upgraded their houses throughout the economic turmoil to skyrocket the value... and it paid off big time.

"But Triguboff, Little, and Mau are seasoned investors! My experience is limited, there's no way I can be a thriving realtor!"

Well, Abhiram and Pavitra will tell you that while experience helps, it doesn't determine your chances of success. You can achieve phenomenal results despite your background, and we've got more stories that will demonstrate why.

Capital Growth of $85,000 in Six Months

Kevin and Pearl lived in Sydney and were looking for attractive investment opportunities. However, they didn't have enough knowledge to choose the right property, so they needed a partner.

That's when they turned to Investors Dream.

One of the most important strategies I taught Kevin and Pearl was to target positive cash flow properties. They're highly beneficial, as they yield higher annual rent than total yearly costs. This can provide a considerable cash surplus before considering depreciation and tax deduction.

Another area Kevin and Pearl were instructed to focus on was high capital growth. The market is rising at a nearly unprecedented rate, so there were ample opportunities to find houses that will increase in value.

On top of that, I wanted them to avoid properties with a high vacancy rate since it suggests they don't rent well. Instead, Kevin and Pearl focused on low-vacancy houses because they're more likely to gain tenants after one vacates the property.

The final pillar of their new approach was to look for properties under market value. In other words, they're sold at a lower price than their actual value. One of the best ways to find these properties is to compare the prices of similar houses in the same region.

These methods may seem overwhelming, but Kevin and Pearl didn't have a hard time mastering them. They now had a clear picture of the right property – the one that would help them transition to real estate seamlessly.

We looked for houses in New South Wales regional areas.

And we didn't find just one property – there were two houses on the same title with tremendous subdivision potential.

The couple bought the properties for $415,000 and immediately started reaping the benefits of positive cash flow. It earns them $278 per week, making their annual recurring income close to $15,000.

The total capital growth is even more impressive. The value of the properties rose by a remarkable $85,000 in just six months.

Although mastering the strategies took some time, it was well worth it for Kevin and Pearl.

Cash Flow of $8,632 in Two Years

Anju and Lokesh are an ambitious couple from Sydney.

They've lived here for 15-20 years, making good money running a home-based childcare and working in the IT sector. Their combined annual income was about $200,000, but they knew they were capable of earning more.

They saw property investment as the best way to improve their financial status.

Initially, the couple planned on expanding their portfolio beyond the sole property they owned in Sydney. They understood that there is great potential to earn good money in this field, but something was holding them back.

They weren't sure where to buy properties and how to remain afloat.

Time was another obstacle. They had two kids and were working full-time jobs. They thought they could never succeed as realtors with so much on their plate.

But their outlook changed once they got in touch with the Investors Dream.

They were inspired by my story, as we came from a similar background. They were basically in the same place I was 15 years ago and were motivated by my achievements in real estate.

Anju and Lokesh discovered that I had a perfect service for people like them. That's when they joined the Investors Dream. In fact, they were my first clients.

The first step on their journey was to expand their knowledge of property investing. They learned the best practices of real estate investing and how to use them in real life.

My go-to methods were at the core of their learning – positive cash flow, high capital growth, low vacancy rate, and buying under market value.

It didn't take them long before they started realising their financial goals.

They bought their first property near Brisbane in December of 2019. The house on a 450 square-metre lot cost $473,000.

This proved to be a remarkable investment. It generated $4,888 of annual cash flow with capital growth of $137,000 in just two years.

But Anju and Lokesh didn't stop there. They looked for more fantastic opportunities and found one in regional NSW.

In March of 2021, they bought a property on a 696-square-metre land for $350,000. It was purchased off the market, and delivered $3,744 in cash flow per year. Capital growth stands at $30,000 (8.6%) in just six months.

The combined cash flow from these investments puts them at nearly $9,000 a year, and their capital growth is an impressive $167,000.

Despite their initial qualms about real estate, Anju and Lokesh quickly found their footing.

A 23-Year Old Landscaper With a Capital Growth of $67,000 in Seven Months

A lot of people start investing in real estate at a young age, hoping to retire by the time they're 35.

But this is what usually happens after a few years...

When they start earning way more than any of their friends, they get tempted to go out and buy fancy stuff. They want to flex their hard-earned money, which is not a bad thing, but they start to lose sight of the prize. As a result, their supposedly early retirement gets delayed.

Many young people fall into this trap, but not Kurt.

He was just 23 when he took up real estate. He was highly inspired by the success of his grandfather, who was also a property investor. Kurt wanted to replicate his results.

He had a clear vision of his goal and worked hard to achieve it.

Kurt had saved a sizeable deposit ($75K) from his stint as a landscaper. This was enough to make his first moves in real estate, but he lacked the necessary education.

He looked for a reliable buyer agent to help him purchase the right investment property. This was when he discovered the Investors Dream.

He contacted us through social media, and we were impressed by his financial acumen.

Kurt had saved a lot of money, which was rare for such a young man. He had resisted the urge to buy boy toys (a boat, camper, or Land Cruiser).

Another admirable thing about Kurt was that he stayed in his parents' home to avoid the hefty costs of renting. Many people in a relationship at this age want to move out of the family home. But Kurt realised this would go against his property investment goals.

Instead, he was determined to find success in real estate first, before sticking it out on his own.

We were eager to help such an ambitious young man, but we had to make sure his first property was foundational. It would be the base of this portfolio, so there was very little room for error.

Fortunately, the search for the right property didn't take long.

Kurt purchased his first house in regional NSW in 2021. He bought the place for $372,000. It was an off the market property with a 772 square-metre lot.

And the purchase couldn't have been better.

Kurt bought the house under market value, which helped deliver huge capital growth of $67,000 in just seven months. It also had a low vacancy rate and tremendous granny flat potential.

On top of that, the cash flow was terrific – $118 per week ($6,136 per year).

Kurt's story debunks another misconception associated with real estate – you can't start property investment in your 20s.

Most young investors would avoid spending so much money due to inexperience, but Kurt was different. He wasn't beating around the bush, as he knew exactly what he was looking for.

As a result, he had obtained valuable education that helped him select an ideal property.

So, if you're thinking you're too young to start investing in property, then you've got to change that mindset. Kurt's story tells us that anyone can accomplish phenomenal results in property investment regardless of age.

After all, what matters more is financial wisdom and proper education.

Real Estate Isn't About Your Background – It's About Making the Right Moves

"Anything's possible if you put your mind to it."

You've probably heard this saying many times.

You might even consider this a platitude, but it has practical implications, especially in property investment.

Each success story you've read above embodies this mindset.

Abhiram and Pavitra desperately wanted to have another stream of income and wealth in Australia before returning to India. The couple is still in their late 30s, and they wanted the choice so in case they themselves or their kids ever came back to Australia; then they wouldn't have to start all over again in this beautiful country.

They didn't know where to start, but the essential ingredient was in place – they had the right mindset.

They didn't want to give up until they created a robust portfolio, and their determination paid off. With guidance from the Investors Dream, they've made excellent purchases and are on the right track to achieving their dreams.

The same goes for Kurt, a young landscaper who followed in his grandfather's footsteps. Many experts would discourage him from investing at 23, but that's not what we did.

We showed him how to purchase the perfect first property. His financial savvy and mindset made this much easier. In fact, he later educated and convinced his own parents to invest in property and they also bought two investment properties with the help of Investors Dream.

But what did Abhiram, Pavitra, Kurt, and other clients have in common?

They recognised that they had so much more to learn before being successful property investors. That's why they joined the Investors Dream.

It helped them build upon their mindset and showed them various options available in the real estate market. Hence, they could now choose a suitable property to invest in, depending on their risk profile.

Another advantage they had was access to the seasoned team of Investors Dream, which consists of experienced professionals with a profound understanding of the market.

Our clients relied on the team's culture, sharing this knowledge to make informed decisions and avoid costly mistakes. Plus, we share the same passion for property investment as our customers, which is why we're eager to help.

CHAPTER 2

From Zero-Knowledge to a Multi-Million Dollar Portfolio in Five Years (Who Am I and Why Should You Listen to Me?)

Many successful property investors never imagined themselves working in this industry when they were little.

That includes me.

I was born in a small town in India, where I had a carefree childhood. I played cricket with my friends and ran along the streets without a worry in my mind.

Growing up, my parents faced incredible hardship. They didn't even finish school. Nevertheless, they worked hard so my siblings and I could go to a good school. Needless to say, our parents ensured we wouldn't go through a difficult ordeal just like they did.

That is why, despite their lack of education, my parents' financial situation turned out to be excellent. My father had a small business, wherein he worked tirelessly to bring home the bacon.

While we couldn't afford fancy clothes or cars, we had an enjoyable life.

As a kid, I felt some pressure to meet my parent's expectations and make sure their efforts didn't go to waste. Still, I had no specific goals. I didn't even have any idea what my profession would be. I couldn't imagine myself in any kind of job, let alone investing in properties.

However, my perspective started to shift as I gained more understanding of business.

I saw the success my father had with his shop.

I knew the money was good.

We never ran out of money to pay our bills.

And my family could afford things that are inaccessible to millions of people in India.

I thought to myself:

"Maybe I could run my own business one day."

But as I grew up watching my dad closely, I also started to recognise the downsides of being a business owner.

My father practically worked 24/7 with no days off. He didn't have any time to spend with the family or go on a vacation with us.

This didn't sound like an ideal life for me, so I tried looking for other career opportunities. One such opportunity presented itself when I took a closer look at the customers visiting my father's shop.

I noticed that some of them weren't well-off, but they also didn't work as much as my father did. They took 1-2 days off every week and even went on two-week holiday during the festival season. Consequently, they had more time for their family, which I thought was pretty cool.

Still, I didn't jump into entrepreneurship right away. Instead, I decided to invest in my education. I took up computer science at a university and wanted to become a software engineer.

Establishing a Thriving Career Out of College

Studying computer science proved to be the right call at the time. The demand for computer engineers was high in the late 1990s, meaning there was plenty of room to land a great job.

Still, I can't say the whole idea of owning my own business completely left my mind at this point. I rented an apartment near my college, and I kept thinking the owner must be rich, as they were regularly getting a large number of rental offers.

That thought lingered in my mind for years, until I finally graduated and found employment in a large business in India. After only two years of working there, my company sent me on a six-month assignment to Australia.

That's how I came to the land down under – with nothing more than a work visa. Honestly, entrepreneurship was the farthest thing from my mind during this time.

After all, my career was thriving. I worked hard, but not to the point of exhaustion. I still had enough time for my family and other social activities.

The income was also excellent. I was delighted to finally fulfil most of my childhood dreams, such as buying a car.

Additionally, I saved up some extra money to help my friends and family.

Life was fantastic.

But it got even better.

My six-month assignment in Australia turned into a two-year job. One thing led to another, and I was offered a permanent position in 2009.

I married and settled in Sydney the same year.

Rekindling an Old Flame

Now, although I had landed an excellent job and married a lovely wife, there was one thing left on my bucket list – and that was to buy a place in India.

I wanted to have my own place should I ever decide to return to my homeland in the future. My parents would surely welcome me into their home, but I didn't want to trouble them. Especially now that I was already making my own money.

I also wanted a safety net for me and my wife. I wanted the assurance that even if I lose my job, I could still rely on the property in India for income.

So, after spending years fantasising about starting my own business and becoming a property investor, I decided to finally take my shot.

I scoured the Indian real estate market until I found the perfect place.

I bought it for an equivalent of $50,000 AUD. It proved to be an excellent purchase, as the house is now worth more than $100,000 AUD.

It might have been beginner's luck, but the windfall made me think:

"Maybe I should reconsider my career path. I bought this property with no investment knowledge, and I can now sell it for twice as much money."

From wondering how rich my landlord in college must have been, my fascination with the real estate industry now grew more than ever.

I loved the idea of earning passive income. As I mentioned earlier, the only thing I didn't like about my father's career as a businessman was that he never seemed to have enough time for himself—or the family.

That's why I was fascinated with passive income. Rather than toiling away to earn money, you sit back and let the funds come your way. In other words, you make money whether or not you're employed.

So, even though I was happy with my job, I couldn't shake the feeling that working for money might not be my best strategy. After all, I despised the idea of exhausting myself for money.

Making One Careful Investing Decision After Another

After finding success with my first-ever property investment, I decided to slowly expand my portfolio. I knew that if I were to make this work, I had to be smart with every decision I made.

So, before making a single investment decision, I made sure to think ten times and research as best as I could, to ensure I was making the right move.

For instance, my wife and I considered whether we should buy or rent a place in Sydney. I compared the numbers and determined that buying houses sometimes doesn't make sense. The mortgage is often higher than the rent, so there was no reason we shouldn't rent for now.

The rest of my journey until 2013 was also marked by prudent real estate deals. I bought another property in India. This one was commercial, and most of the financing came from my funds. I did have to borrow a small amount of money from a friend, but the interest was reasonable.

This property was an excellent move, too. It generated a lot of positive cash flow, offering a stable source of income.

After the second purchase, my wife and I started thinking about buying a place in Australia. By 2014, we had already settled and made tremendous headway in our jobs. It was time to buy something for ourselves.

We did so in 2014. It was a place in Western Sydney that required no renovations. We finally had our dream house, and it took a huge burden off our shoulders – we no longer had to rent.

We were thrilled about the purchase, but this didn't stop us from pursuing real estate opportunities.

Toward the end of 2014, we bought an apartment with a credit card balance transfer. The market in Sydney was going in the right direction, meaning we could expect the value of the property to increase.

Moreover, the location of the apartment was highly attractive. It was near a railway station and the Westfield Shopping Centre.

Another thing going in our favour was that we bought the unit in the first release of a very big development project. First release properties are always cheaper, so we purchased the place under market value.

The total investment set us back $350,000. Only six months later, the property's value skyrocketed to $420,000.

The $70,000 uptick made us ecstatic. The best part is that we achieved it without virtually any property investment knowledge.

But why was my property investment knowledge limited?

Because I simply couldn't focus on real estate. After all, I was still spending most of my time at my day job.

Transitioning Out of Corporate

Despite my incredible early success in real estate investing, I wasn't thinking of becoming a full-time investor just yet.

That decision came a little later—when my parents paid me a visit in Australia. They were proud of me for having settled in this country since it offered a better quality of life compared with India.

But they also told me that my wife and I should visit them more frequently because they wouldn't be able to move to Australia.

This was a serious pain point for me.

I was climbing the ladder in my corporate job and was making decent money. But as I took on higher and higher positions, I was left with less and less free time.

This made me realise:

"If my parents needed me to come to India, I wouldn't even have time to do so."

This was the exact scenario I wanted to avoid. I didn't want to be successful in my career at the expense of my family, so I looked for a way out. Working in IT was no longer viable for me, so I finally considered making real estate my full-time job.

Finally Taking the Leap Towards Full-Time Property Investing

This idea of going full-time in real estate was reinforced in 2015—the year my daughter was born. My wife and I were too busy with our jobs, so we signed our daughter up for childcare.

I was heartbroken when I found out she cried nearly all the time when we were not around. This was unacceptable to me.

My emotions overwhelmed me. I realised this wasn't the life I had dreamed of. I didn't even have enough time for my daughter. I couldn't hold onto my job forever.

I turned to the field where I felt more at home – property investment.

Other people were quitting their jobs and becoming realtors. Nothing was stopping me from doing the same.

I was more motivated because I wanted to free up my schedule for my family. I was inspired by people who retired after working just 5-10 years at property investment. This became my goal.

The funds earned from my IT job covered my basic expenses and provided income to purchase investment properties.

I started learning about property intensively in 2015. I had some practical experience, but it wasn't enough to accomplish serious results.

Sometimes, I was too afraid to take action.

Other times, I couldn't find the right property since I didn't know what to look for.

Education was my game-changer. I used to think you had to buy dozens of properties per year to earn a decent income, but that's not the case.

I learned you could just buy one or two houses annually and still build a decent property portfolio and earn your living. And one of the best ways to do that is to invest in positive cash flow properties and make use of different available structures to be able to buy multiple properties. It's a reliable source that allows you to supplement your income and create a large portfolio much faster.

I picked up many other valuable strategies, all of which helped me set a clear goal.

In the next five years, I wanted to be in a position to leave my job without any repercussions. My goal was to generate $100,000 in passive income so that I could retire and have all the time in the world for my family.

Once I started learning and taking actions, I realised there was no need to postpone my investment despite serviceability issues. My daughter had just been born, and my wife wouldn't go back to work for the next 9-10 months.

We only had about $20,000 in cash, but this was enough for a joint venture deal.

My Joint Venture partnerand I bought a property for $85,000 with tremendous subdivision potential. It was an excellent opportunity because we could build two houses on each lot after the subdivision.

It was also a low-risk investment since the price was relatively low.

After paying the stamp duty, each subdivision cost us $50,000. The services were already there, so it was cheap.

My Joint Venture partner sold his property for $75,000, earning him a quick $25,000 profit.

I didn't want to let go of my property just yet, which turned out to be a smart decision. I kept my 600 square metres of land and built a house with granny flat potential. This set me back $410,000.

You might be thinking: "Why would you build a granny flat rather than a standard house?"

The answer is simple – it was more affordable.

Everyone else constructed standard four-bedroom houses, but few people could afford them. I wanted to offer something cheaper to ensure a low vacancy rate and higher profitability.

This move paid off. I'm renting it out for $780 per week, and it's delivering $14,000 in positive cash flow.

It was an amazing deal, but I worked hard to find it.

I must have checked out more than 100 properties in the area. I also hired a town planner and land server for their advice. Moreover, I often called the council to obtain key information about interesting houses.

Therefore, I pulled off this fantastic deal because I leveraged the expertise of other people. I was relatively new to the industry, so I didn't have much to work with. My solution was to follow the advice of others to discover profitable properties.

For example, I would never have learned that this lot was already subdivided if I hadn't contacted an expert. They reached out to the council and land office on my behalf, asking them to reinitiate the old title. This would allow me to purchase the property for a lower price.

The old title was reinitiated, and the only expense I had to cover was $2,000 to the land surveyor. This was when I discovered you should always dig deep for incredible deals and rely on others, especially if you're just getting started.

Another thing I learned during this deal is that you shouldn't hesitate. It was strange that the owner would sell a property with so much upside. Many would try to figure out their motivations, but that's not what I did.

Instead, I performed my due diligence, working out if I should proceed with the purchase. The numbers checked out, so there was no reason to delay the deal.

And it didn't matter that this was a small deal. I never intended to make a boatload of money – my primary goal was not to lose money and learn the process.

Even if I made a mistake, it wouldn't bankrupt me. I would still have enough money for another deal.

The granny flat property was an icebreaker. I understood how joint ventures work and that limited funds aren't a problem if you have the right mindset.

I continued to educate myself, amassing knowledge for my next purchase. It delivered even better results than the previous purchase.

I bought a property for $300,000 and spent $50,000 on renovations. The land had excellent potential for subdivision and the construction of another house.

Although the house was far away from my residence (150 kilometres), this didn't discourage me from the renovations. The location was great, as the place was in a large regional town with a good population and solid infrastructure.

I'm now running this property as a standard family house, renting it out for $470 per week.

Shortly afterwards, I purchased another property. There were three titles on the house, and the price was only $323,000.

In addition, subdividing the land was easy. It was a 1,270 square-metre lot, with 400 square metres as the minimum size necessary to build another house. Hence, I could easily construct two more properties.

The original house was the main highlight of this purchase, though. It was a standard property that required no renovations. I bought it under market value in an attractive location (town centre), and I'm renting it out for $350 per week and worth around $600,000 after 4 years.

The Common Ground Across All My Deals

This brings me to a common thread in all my deals – positive cash flow.

The first property generated $14,000, whereas the second one eclipsed it. The third house didn't provide as much cash flow, but it contributed to my stable finances.

I was hell-bent on achieving my goal, which was earning $100,000 in passive income or at least $2 million in equity. These positive cash flow properties were the most effective way to accomplish it.

While there were many commonalities in my real estate strategies, I switched things up from time to time.

At one point, I transitioned some of my investments into a room-by-room model rather than renting them out to a family. This method was in line with my passive income objective.

I looked for positive-cash flow properties, and I heard about rooming houses in Victoria and other parts of New South Wales. I thought this was my winning lottery ticket.

I calculated that setting up just one of these properties could generate $50,000-$60,000 in positive cash flow. The demand was high since rooms are more affordable than houses.

Like all my investments, I started small. I bought a four-room property to learn the process, allowing me to transition to larger projects over time.

The results were solid. I earned a decent amount of positive cash flow, but I soon discovered the downside of my approach. The properties were too far from Sydney, meaning I couldn't manage them on my own.

I hired real estate agents, which limited the control over my investment and generated unnecessary expenses.

Nevertheless, this didn't prevent me from creating a robust portfolio.

I have two properties in India, completely paid off and ten more in Australia, including my principal place of residence (PPR). I want to expand my portfolio, and these twelve properties have been a terrific starting point.

I plan on constructing a few properties pending approval, and I want to keep buying houses across Australia. I've learned a lot over the years and have plenty of time to invest successfully.

Paying it Forward

With so much experience and so many deals under my belt, I decided to help other property investors. That's why I founded the Investors Dream.

I've always enjoyed helping my friends – I was their go-to person for real estate advice. I also noticed a huge gap in the market, where most investors are first-time buyers. They had no representation, increasing the risk of buying the wrong properties, in the wrong locations at the wrong time.

Uneducated people rarely thrive in this field, but that's where the Investors Dream comes into play. I want to help investors avoid the pitfalls I faced during my career and help them save time and money.

Another motivator was that helping other people wasn't time-consuming. I could still focus on my own portfolio while pointing our clients in the right direction.

My role in the Investors Dream is to be a buyer agent. I help the investors buy investment properties and grow their portfolio over time.

Unfortunately, many beginners face this problem.

They don't have the proper education and can't take action. It takes them too long to make a decision. By the time they want to pull the trigger, the opportunity is gone.

What's more, newbie investors typically have doubts about real estate. They've embarked on their journey, but they still think making big bucks is impossible.

My mission is to change their mindset.

If you're one of these people, I want you to invest in yourself before investing in property. Listen to successful people and don't bide your time. The most important thing is to get started, do the numbers, and only purchase neutral to positive cash flow properties to start with.

Those are just some of the lessons I can teach you at the Investors Dream. The experience accumulated through my education and deals has enabled me to help others follow the same path to success and wealth as me.

The next chapter will tell you more about this path. You'll gain insights into my framework – property investment fundamental principles.

CHAPTER 3

The Different Stages of Your Property Investment Journey

Several factors should be considered in starting one's property investing journey. For example, you should look into your personal risk appetite, your level of financial education, and what your goals are for investing in the first place.

While there is no "one size fits all" strategy to successful property investment, it's important for you as a property investor to understand what can influence your decisions as you progress.

Through my own property journey and learning, I discovered different stages of property investing. These are the stages that every property investor has to go through on their way to achieving their passive income goals, and more.

Knowing these stages will help you plan ahead to better accomplish your property investment goals. Especially since you will encounter different contexts or challenges as you move forward.

Through this chapter, you will learn that self-education, doing the right things and taking action can go a long way to achieving financial independence.

The Stages of Your Property Journey

A property investor usually goes through a four-stage life cycle, which will be discussed in detail shortly. These four stages of property investment serve as a guide not just for beginners, but also for long-time investors.

But before you can fully embrace the journey ahead, you need to start by purchasing your first property. Think of this as a qualifying game that happens before the main tournament.

As you move towards getting your first property, the main thing you need to remember is that it is a process.

At this point, you have yet to acquire the property. Hence, as a potential buyer, you must work towards the deal by learning everything you can about property and acquiring the financial resources to seal the deal.

So, ask yourself questions like:

What is the outcome you're after with this purchase? What's your plan with this property? This is especially important if you want to make the most out of your purchase. Also, do you want to do some renovations? And are you thinking of subdividing or constructing a new structure on the property or simply buy and hold it for a longer term?

If you're really set on a particular property, make sure that you have enough money to pay the initial deposit and associated costs, as well as any additional costs, particularly if you are planning to renovate or subdivide. This way, it'll be easier for you to secure and complete the intended work on that property.

Now, if you have a limited budget, you can always choose to set a price range you're comfortable with and only look at properties within that range. But keep in mind that you also need to think about stamp duty and other expenses like legal fees and building inspections.

Another factor to be considered when purchasing a property is the location. Its effect on property values can vary, depending on a number of external factors.

For instance, if the area where the property is situated has a thriving local economy and features government offices, transportation hubs, and other vital institutions, you can expect that the property prices for that area will be very high.

In a similar fashion, demographic changes in the area can also have an impact on future prices. An increase in the youth population in an area can be positive since their presence could increase the demand for transport links, housing prices, and amenities.

Researching a property will allow you to avoid overvaluing it. This is very important, especially if you are just starting to build a property investment portfolio. Without doing proper research, you risk making less than you expect.

With that in mind, it must be noted that land does not depreciate. So, if you are purchasing a house with a decent land component to it, chances are that its market value will increase over time.

Likewise, timing is also important. Buying properties at its bottom or in a moving market that has not yet peaked, for example, can help give you a boost to capital growth in the shorter term, and to your confidence in investing.

Always think about how your first property purchase will help acquire your second—and even third—investment property. Remember that each purchase should help you move forward.

As mentioned, purchasing your first property is just one step in your entire investment journey. Once you've done that, you can then focus on your second property, then the third, and so on. Property investing is an ongoing process of planning, implementing, reviewing and repeating.

Let us look at the four stages you'll encounter next in your investment journey.

Stage #1. Accumulation

In the accumulation stage, you need to focus on purchasing properties and growing your property portfolio. These properties should be in high-growth locations for you to have enough equity built in both the short term and the long term. At the same time, your property investments should generate enough cash flow so your portfolio remains sustainable in case something goes wrong in your personal or professional life.

Once you get rental income from your investment property, you can then focus on expanding your portfolio. This means investing in as many properties as you can afford while holding on to your existing properties and being able to pay the mortgages and outgoings comfortably.

In this stage, either you have one or ten properties.

It is very important to have enough cash buffer in place for any unforeseen circumstances or any changes in the rate of interest. This way, you won't end up selling any of your properties unwillingly.

You must always remind yourself to keep accumulating properties at a pace you're comfortable with in this stage. Invest as long as you have enough savings, borrowing power and enough cash buffer. There's no point waiting to buy an investment property when you can buy now.

Always remember, property investing is all about time in the market, rather than timing the market.

So, purchase as much real estate as you can without going overboard. But make sure your cash flow from these properties is always positive or neutral. Worst case, it's slightly negative in exceptional circumstances, such as when the rate of interest is much higher than usual.

If you want to keep moving forward, investing in high-growth properties with neutral or positive cash flow is essential.

This stage is very crucial for a property investor. As such, you need a great team of professionals all the time so you can get the right advice and timely support—whether it be in buying a property or deciding on a purchasing entity or restructuring finance.

Take note that since land appreciates over time, you will also be able to increase rent in relation to the appreciation of assets. And as mentioned, macro and micro economic factors can play a huge part in the appreciation of the property, so you have to keep them in mind.

Another concept to remember at this stage is to avoid making emotional or irrational judgments in acquiring or developing properties. You have to be scientific in your investments, which means you must make investment decisions based on facts and figures, not feelings.

Stage #2. Consolidation

In this stage, your aim as a property investor is to minimise the overall debt of your property portfolio. This is about lowering your loan-to-value ratio and increasing cash flow as much as possible.

This stage usually takes place around a couple of years before you want to retire from your active employment. Note that there is no specific age for retirement since this varies depending on the person. Only you will be able to determine if you want to enter this stage and when.

At this stage, you can start winding down the purchase of properties and simply let things grow on their own. You can even sell a few of your properties to reduce debt, then use the profit from these sales to further reduce debt and eventually increase rental cash flow.

This stage is also more of a reflection of how far you have come on your property investing journey since you started. It's also time to celebrate those decisions you made in the past for you and your loved ones.

As such, the best strategy at this point includes the restructuring of any debts to eliminate personal debt, such as the mortgage on your own home, if you have one. You can try increasing the mortgage on an investment property and paying off the mortgage on your own home.

You may also look into moving any investment purchases made under your name to your family structure for asset protection, land tax optimisation or income distribution, in case they were not purchased under the correct structure. Ideally, have your property portfolio reviewed by your team of experts before you make any necessary changes to optimise the outcome.

Stage #3. Generating Passive Income

Once you reach the stage where you're able to generate passive income, you can start living comfortably off the revenue flow from your portfolio.

It's also at this stage where you're finally seeing the tangible results of your property investments, as well as reaping all the efforts you put in during the accumulation and consolidation stages.

In a way, this is when you can look back to why you started your property investment journey: to generate enough money and supplement (or replace) the money you make at work.

At this stage in your journey, you also have a new set of options available to you.

For example, you could decide to pay off all the loans in your portfolio and only rely on passive income to support yourself. But keep in mind that if you do that, you'll lose out on the tax and leverage benefits. Of course, this still is a great situation to be in because there won't be any financial strain on your portfolio.

If you prefer to go a less cautious path, you can pay down the debt you incurred with your property portfolio to get the best loan-to-value ratio. In doing so, you'll continue to earn a fantastic passive income while retaining some tax advantages and leverage.

Stage #4. The Legacy

The final phase of every property investment journey is retirement and creating your legacy. It is at this stage where you have achieved your financial freedom and independence through property investing.

This means you have a solid property investment portfolio and your savings and money are at a good level.

As such, you can now afford the kind of lifestyle you want for yourself and your family. You're also free to pursue the activities you want without being driven by a set salary each month.

What's more, all your existing liabilities derived from purchasing and developing your properties have all been fully paid off. You are now able to focus on capital gains—that is, you'll be able to live off the surplus rents.

In other words, there are no more bank deductibles to your rent since there are no more existing liabilities.

But here's the interesting thing:

This stage is where you can begin asking yourself how you want to use your money to create an impact on those around you.

Of course, you can use the money you've earned for yourself. But if you think about it deeper, there's so much that you can do. For example, you can use your portfolio to ensure your family's financial security in the years to come. You could also help organisations or charities.

When you've been investing in real estate for a while, you might start to reflect on your accomplishments. And you'll eventually realise that there is no feeling that compares to the pleasure and sense of success you get from knowing that you have the ability to contribute something good to your community.

Know that the legacy stage is a "fluid state," to use the terminology of some seasoned investors.

This implies that you are free to do whatever you want with your possessions. Interestingly, when property investors get to this point, they frequently start accumulating again.

To be clear, it's perfectly okay to re-enter the property investment game and start at stage one again. But I'm of the belief that it's better to leave something behind so that others remember you in the future.

Because of this, it's best for you to carefully consider the retirement and legacy stage and develop a plan that works for you and your family. Not only that, you also have to create a way for you to spread your impact and help more people.

In doing so, you can be remembered by future generations this way:

You're not just a property investor but someone who made decisions that aligned with their values.

CHAPTER 4

The Property Quartet

Tom and Crystal are busy people.

He works as a general manager and she works as an executive assistant. On top of making good income from their corporate jobs… the couple already have a beautiful home and one investment property in Sydney. In other words—they were happy and well-provided for.

As such, Tom and Crystal never viewed property investing as something they *absolutely* have to do. It's never been about finding a get-rich-quick scheme for these two. Instead, they *wanted* to make more sound investments in property in order to create more wealth and secure their future the best way possible.

This gave Tom and Crystal the luxury of time to interview a lot of buyers' agents in search for one who can grow their portfolio the way they would. They wanted to make sure they were working with someone who has a solid framework of strategies. Strategies that can help them build wealth consistently and for the long run.

So, after dozens of agent interviews, they signed up with us. Within eight months of applying the same set of strategies I'll be sharing with you in this chapter… they were able to buy four properties and again after a year they bought their fifth property.

Their first investment was worth $398,000. The Adelaide property is now worth $490,000… translating to a capital growth of 23% in 14 months.

Their second investment cost them $420,000. The property, located in regional NSW, is now worth $510,000. That's a 21% capital growth in just twelve months.

Their third investment, also in regional NSW, was worth $374,000. After a bathroom renovation, it's now valued at $450,000, making a 12.5% growth in just twelve months, plus this site has development opportunities.

Their forth investment is in regional QLD purchased at $337,000, immediately rented out for $470/wk and worth $410,000, making a 21.6% growth in 10 months.

Their fifth investment is in metro WA purchased at $525,000, renting out at $600/wk and worth at least $550,000 in just 3 months.

And the best part about all these investments is that Tom and Crystal did not have to reinvent the wheel every time.

They simply relied on **The Property Quartet.** It's a set of four strategies that allowed them to make profitable investments in quick succession.

Those strategies include:

- Finding positive cash flow properties
- Investing for capital growth
- Looking for properties that have potential for value-adding activities
- Buying under actual value

If those strategies sound familiar… that's because it is the same set of strategies that has helped Abhiram and Pavitra, Kurt, Kevin and Pearl… and hundreds of our other clients make profitable investments in less than a year.

Throughout the next chapters, I'll take you along for a deep dive into how these strategies work… and how they can work for *you.*

But for now, let's take a quick look at each one and why I consider them part of the elite property quartet.

Focusing on Positive Cash Flow Properties

All properties of Tom and Crystal's investments involved positive cash flow properties. This means the yearly rent they receive from those properties… is greater than their total yearly expenses.

In other words, those properties are self-sustaining and profitable from day one… leaving you with an income-generating portfolio.

The alternative is to invest in negatively-geared properties… which means your portfolio is draining finances faster than you're earning them.

The positive cash flow strategy forms part of our property quartet… especially for newbie investors who have yet to build their war chest to cover for unforeseen expenses.

An example of a typically positive cash flow property would be the granny flat. Tom and Crystal's second property, which is located in regional NSW, was targeted for this very reason. It has great granny flat potential, which is good for the instant cash flow of a second income.

See, on average, a single-bedroom granny flat would cost you about a hundred thousand bucks. And as you could rent it out for at least $200 to $250 a week, your yield would be around 13% annually. Additionally, you can secure granny flats with several investment strategies like joint ventures. I'll explain more about that in the next chapter.

For now, let's talk about the potential disadvantages of investing in positive cash flow properties. For starters, investing in positively-geared properties will not give you any losses… that you can offset against your personal, taxable income. Additionally, you could be placed into a higher tax bracket, since the income you'd be collecting from the property will, of course, be taxable.

Still, these disadvantages do not hold a candle to the advantages you can enjoy with positive cash flow properties.

After all, cash flow IS the lifeblood of any business.

And in the next chapter, I'll go in depth on how positive cash flow properties improve your cash flow… gives you better serviceability… and gives you a buffer against increases or fluctuations in the interest rates.

I'll also demonstrate why investing specifically in positive cash flow properties help you achieve a strong growth mindset… which will then allow you to expand your portfolio much faster.

These are all the reasons positive cash flow properties are a central part of our investment strategy.

Investing for Capital Growth

All of Tom and Crystal's investments were made in high capital growth areas. This ensures that the value of those properties will increase over time, promising them huge returns on their investment.

Simply put, capital growth is the difference between the price you pay for a property, and its actual market value at any point in the future. After all, it's not just the recurring rental income that we're chasing when investing in property. We also want to look at a strong exit strategy… which means you have to seek price appreciation on the property you're investing in.

As you will learn in more detail come Chapter Six, the increase in the value of a property does not always happen automatically. This means a property may gradually appreciate naturally over time, but there are things you can do to accelerate such value growth… or at least make sure that you're investing in a location that's bound to see growth in the future.

One way you can do this is by following infrastructure developments, like transportation projects… and the expansion of hospitals and universities. These projects drive growth to a certain location.

Another capital growth driver you should take note of would be population growth. See, increases in the population of a particular area is good news for real estate investors… if they catch it early enough.

After all, population growth leads to a higher demand for properties. However, timing is a central piece of this investment strategy. Ideally, you want to get in before developments like infrastructure investments and population growth actually kick in.

Being late to the party means you're already buying properties at an increased rate… defeating the purpose of investing for capital growth.

Now, the challenge here is finding locations that have yet to see its boom. The good news is that infrastructure developments have picked up in the last two years. Population is likewise growing. All you have to do is capitalise on these opportunities using the strategies included in our property quartet.

Chapter Six will give you a more comprehensive discussion on how you can find high capital growth areas… but for now, let's move on to the third investment strategy in our property quartet:

Using Value Add Strategies

There are two parts to using value add strategies in growing your portfolio:

- Finding properties that have yet to reach their full potential
- Doing what it takes for these properties to realise their actual market value

The key thing to understand here is that there could be a dozen different reasons why a certain property has yet to reach its full potential. These include poor management… the need for cash and labor-intensive repairs… and plummeting demand for what the property has to offer.

What you have to do is find properties that are not yet completely doomed… and would thus respond to corrective action to reach their full, actual market value.

For instance, a property that requires massive renovations but is located in a high capital growth location might be a good choice… since you'd still be getting a good return on your investment of cash and sweat.

On the other hand, a property that requires a complete flip… and is located in an area where there is hardly any demand for it might be a lost cause for your portfolio.

Once you've found these diamonds in the rough… you still have the second part of the strategy to think about: doing what it takes to boost these properties so they can reach their full potential.

And that's where the strategies laid out in Chapter Six come into play. These are:

- Cosmetic renovations
- Adding a granny flat
- Subdividing a property
- Taking on new builds

These strategies vary in attractiveness based on your capacity, preferences, and risk appetite. For instance, if you're still in the process of building up capital and connections in the industry… building a granny flat might make more sense than building a larger building.

If you don't mind putting in the sweat equity, renovating can be a great way to increase the rent you can charge for a certain property… or even sell it for a much higher price than you bought it! On the other hand, subdividing a property does not require as much dirty work… but you still have to deal with a lot of bureaucracy and feasibility considerations.

Indeed, there are a lot of things you need to consider before deciding on which value-add strategy works best for you… but that's why I've dedicated an entire chapter to discuss the nitty-gritty of value-add properties for you.

You'd have to read through Chapter Seven for that, but for now… let's wrap up this discussion on the property quartet by looking at the fourth and final strategy:

Buying Under Value

Do you remember Kurt from the previous chapter? At 23 years old, he had saved just enough for his first investment property. And because he didn't want to wait, we went for a property he could buy off the market and under market value.

This is a great strategy, because it means he was able to purchase the property… for less than what the market thinks it should have sold for.

In Chapter Eight, I will give you more examples of how our clients have made a killing by buying properties under value. You will also learn of various strategies to buy below market value… including buying below replacement costs… focusing on established properties… and capitalising on factors that incentivises sellers to sell fast.

However, Chapter Eight will also tell you about the hard work required in buying under value. Since you're not investing heavy equity into these properties… it's only expected that you will make up for it by investing a lot of research and hard work.

You have to leverage market data… uncover the seller's motivation… look for hidden gems… scour older listings… and keep up with auctions just to find properties that you can snag under value.

That said, the biggest investment you might have to make when buying under value is your patience.

You also have to learn how to negotiate terms beyond the actual price of the property. There are some ways you can sweeten the deal for the seller, given that they're selling under market value. Coming up with this win-win situation may be tough at times… but we'll work together on that in the chapters to come.

And that wraps up our discussion on your property investing quartet. The four strategies you've learned in this chapter, albeit challenging, can supercharge your portfolio in the long run. These will ensure that you won't have to go through trial and error, and burn through your capital, trying to reinvent the wheel each time.

The time-tested property quartet of sound investing has delivered fantastic results for both my and my clients' property portfolios… and I'm excited for what they can do to yours. With that, let's go on a deeper dive into each of the strategies one by one.

CHAPTER 5

Cash Flow Is the Lifeblood of Your Business

Let me ask you a question.

Why do you invest in real estate?

Is it merely to collect as many properties as you can? Or is it to make money?

Of course, for many of us, it's the latter.

This is exactly why you shouldn't purchase just any property you could find, because if you buy property you can't sell for profit, well, you'd end up with a collection of properties that aren't making you any money.

Take negatively-geared houses as an example. Many investors purchase these, attracted by the idea of paying lower taxes, but failing to consider other long-term consequences.

Besides having an adverse effect on your cash flow, this strategy of collecting properties regardless of profitability can also influence your mindset negatively.

See, when a property doesn't make you money, all it does is cost you money. And when a property costs you money every day, there's no motivation to continue investing. That's why around 90% of investors only have one property here in Australia, even if they're capable of performing better.

Negative gearing holds them back and keeps them from capitalising on their skills. They've lost sight of their goals and can't get back on track.

The situation is entirely different when you focus on positively-geared properties.

You get positive cash flow that lets you supplement your monthly income more reliably.

And it's not just your finances that benefit from this approach.

It's also your mindset.

When you see a consistent income stream every week, you get to buy more properties and increase your motivation.

You're not slaving away to earn money.

Instead, your investment is generating income for you. Your properties are doing great, which drives you to expand your portfolio.

Finding the right house might require some effort at first, but it comes naturally over time.

Best of all, an income-generating portfolio doesn't put extra pressure on your finances in case of contingencies. The same can’t be said for owners of negatively-geared properties and portfolios.

If they lose their job, their business goes under, or when something like COVID comes along, they don't have any income to overcome the hardship. In fact, they have to invest more money into their property to stay afloat.

That's the main reason these investors stick around for just a few years before selling their portfolios. They lose a ton of money and can't sustain their holding for longer.

The simplest way to avoid this is to buy positive cash flow properties. You're not forced to sell, as you've ensured another source of income. Your portfolio can grow regardless of your job or market changes. This is because you've created a self-sustainable system that requires minimal involvement.

Of course, you can purchase a few negatively-geared properties, but only in the later stages of your journey. You should only buy positive cash flow houses early on since you're taking your first steps. When you're not well-versed in real estate, the last thing you need is to lose motivation by investing in the wrong properties.

This way, you'll be on the right track to accomplishing your property goals. If you're like me, you'll be able to leave your job and enjoy freedom.

To help you better understand why I insist on positive cash flow properties, let's dive into the main benefits of this tactic.

Real Estate Investment Is About Improving Cash Flow

As previously mentioned, a positive cash flow property is usually a self-sustaining property that keeps you from covering any shortfalls from the get-go.

For instance, suppose you purchased a house in a high capital growth zone for about $480,000. You rent the place out for $550 per week, and there's an interest-only mortgage that amounts to $20,000 per year. Your annual expenses are approximately $5,000, meaning your rent covers the costs and generates a profit.

That's the most significant advantage of investing in these properties. You get cash from the start you can use to cover unforeseen expenses and debt, making this strategy perfect for newbie investors.

Another way you can use this cash is to pay off your mortgage quicker and grow your portfolio faster.

Furthermore, your borrowing capacity improves since banks consider your finances more stable. You can also obtain various capital gains, as the value of your property should rise if you make the right purchase. On average, cash flow positive houses produce about 7% of capital growth every year.

Although this approach doesn't require a lot of involvement, this doesn't mean you should sit idle. There are many ways to maximise your cash flow:

- Increasing rent – This is the most common way of improving cash flow. You can perform it by acquiring under-performing properties (the rent is lower than the market demand) and adjusting the lease to your market rent. Alternatively, you can revamp the house, install new amenities (e.g., a dishwasher and central AC) or improve the cosmetic finish to raise the rent.

- Long-term tenants – Vacancy and turnover can kill your cash flow, so you should prevent this at all costs. You want to keep your tenants happy with your amenities to ensure they're in for the long term. Plus, you should respond to maintenance requests quickly and increase rents according to market conditions when the lease expires.

- Preventative maintenance – Your cash flow can be wiped out for months due to large maintenance and repair expenses. Preventative measures can safeguard against this. Some of the jobs you should do are clean out the gutters before winter, trim trees close to the property, and take care of the HVAC unit. Thinking ahead allows you to avoid unpleasant surprises.

- Refinancing – You may want to consult your lender occasionally and stay on top of the mortgage interest rate. If it's falling, you might be eligible for refinancing to lower the mortgage and increase cash flow. However, make sure to factor in closing and lender fees to determine if the strategy is worth it.

Before increasing your cash flow, you'll need to have some cash flow to start with. This requires you to purchase a property, but which ones should you target?

Dual living houses and duplexes are a great way to have positive cash flow instantly. They look like individual homes but feature separate entrances. Also, the inside comprises two dwellings – one usually has three bedrooms, whereas the other doesn't have more than two.

As for the price, these properties go for upwards of $500,000. Tenants like their modern look, and they typically have lower rents than standalone houses. Additionally, these houses don't have strata fees and are normally in high-demand areas. If you lose a tenant in one part, the other tenant will still pay rent.

Throughout this book, I've mentioned another type of property you should target for positive cash flow – granny flats. They're ideal for obtaining instant cash flow and a secondary income.

You can build your granny flats for around $100,000 - $200,000 depending upon the material and quality of build, and you can rent them out for at least $300-$400 per week. In terms of the yield, you can expect around $10K-12K per year.

Duplex houses can even have subdivision potential. Look for these properties since they can not only boost your cash flow but equity as well.

A subdivision lets you build two houses, enabling you to charge two rents. Still, don't rely on this strategy if you've never invested. Stick to one property per lot until you're more familiar with the process.

You could also focus on properties for the disabled. The government has allocated $700 million annually through the NDIS to provide affordable housing for these people. The private sector will carry out this project, and the rent allowances can provide up to 12% in annual return. This is a great opportunity to set up a positive cash flow property.

Apart from selecting a suitable property, you need to do some math to determine if it generates positive cash flow. The 1% rule will help you do that.

According to this rule, you've likely found a positive cash flow place if the rent is at least 1% of its purchase price.

Here's an example to clarify the principle.

Let's say you bought a house for $100,000 with a monthly rent of $1,000. This means you've found an appropriate property because the cash flow is 1% of the purchase price.

Now, even though this property passed the 1% test, you shouldn't sign the contract and buy it right away. Many other details need to check out:

- Property taxes
- Mortgage
- Insurance
- Vacancy
- Repairs
- Strata Fee (if applicable)

It's essential to analyse each factor because it can make or break your chances of success. If you overlook an expense or two, you might be in for an unpleasant surprise at the end of the month.

Let's take a look at an example of how much cash flow you can obtain after considering all these aspects:

- The price of the property is $500,000.
- The weekly rent is $600, making the yearly amount just over $31,200 with a 2% vacancy rate.
- Your loan interest is $13,000 in the first year, and other expenses are $4,120. This means your pre-tax flow is $14,080.
- The non-cash deductions (fittings and property depreciation) and loan costs are $7,500 in the first year.

With a little more than $31,000 in your income and $24,000 in expenses, your on-paper profit in the first year is $7,000.

Now, let's assume that your cash flow after taxation is just $22 per week ($1,079) in the first year. You might think this is too little to grow your portfolio, but you're forgetting a crucial detail – your cash flow rises over time.

Whether your vacancy rate is lower or you've increased your rent, the following years will be much more profitable. Here's how your cash flow can look in the next 5-10 years:

- Year 1 – $22 of positive cash flow per week
- Year 2 – $32 of positive cash flow per week
- Year 3 – $35 of positive cash flow per week
- Year 5 – $48 of positive cash flow per week
- Year 10 – $84 of positive cash flow per week

Again, $84 per week may not seem much, but it's still a solid amount of money going into your pocket after covering all expenses. Meanwhile, the value of your property is rising and may even double after a decade.

This allows you to accumulate $500,000, skyrocketing your profit.

The question you should ask now is: does this align with my goal? Is this the cash flow I wanted to generate with my property?

Keep in mind that the amount of cash flow investors are happy with varies. It's heavily influenced by the market, and finding positive cash flow houses in certain markets is extremely hard. But if you can find your hidden gem, you can create admirable cash flow with high rents.

Vice-versa, you might be able to effortlessly find appropriate properties in cooler markets. However, the rents are generally too low to move your financial needle.

Property values and local rates also play a significant role in positive cash flow.

For example, say your friend purchased a beachfront property that generates positive cash flow. The cash flow is about $2,000 per month after clearing all expenses. The rent is high, allowing them to score a huge profit.

At the same time, let's say you bought a house in a not-so-attractive location. You charge less for the rent and receive just $800 in cash flow per month. You might think your friend outperformed you, but is that really the case?

The chances are their beachfront property was incomparably costlier than your house. You spent much less money to buy your place, which probably means your cash-on-cash return was higher.

This example highlights that you shouldn't look strictly at your cash flow. You also need to consider the return on investment (ROI), risk tolerance, market, and priorities. All of which are vital to expanding your portfolio.

Positive Cash Flow Improves Serviceability

Serviceability is your ability to borrow more money. The more money you can borrow, the more properties you can buy to expand your portfolio and generate cash flow.

But how do lenders calculate your serviceability? Most use a basic formula.

Your gross income is the starting point. From there, a number of elements are deducted, such as tax, existing and new commitments, a buffer, and living expenses. What's left is your surplus (the money you can use to pay off your mortgage).

The factors considered can vary from bank to bank, but here's what lenders generally analyse when determining your serviceability:

- Annual income
- Monthly expenses
- Interest rate
- Your loan type
- Repayment structure (interest and principal, or only interest)
- Loan term

- Monthly repayments

Keep in mind that banks will require proof of income. This usually includes your recent payslips, tax returns, and any BAS statements if you're a business owner. Plus, they may request your credit card statements or bank account.

On top of that, they'll subtract costs and liabilities from your post-taxation income, like other loans or credit card debt.

They'll also include a buffer to the interest rate to account for future increases.

Up until two years ago, lenders would normally use at least 7% as the buffer interest rates.

But as the rates are dropping, they determined this to be needlessly high. They amended the criterion to reflect the ongoing changes more accurately.

Nowadays, banks generally add margins of approximately 2%-2.5% to your rate to judge your serviceability.

Let's see what this means in practice.

If you apply for a $450,000 loan with a 5% interest rate, your ability to repay the loan will be assessed according to a higher rate. Rather than 5%, it will be closer to 7%-8%.

It's also worth noting that your income analysis may consist of more than your regular salary. It can comprise overtime, bonuses, commissions, and shift allowances. Some industries (e.g., police, nursing and fire services) might be obligated to provide these details because they encounter them more often.

If you own a few properties (including your home), the bank considers your rental income. Other critical details include mortgage repayment, utilities, rates, bills, and other liabilities. You should also remember that lenders normally consider a portion of your income only when figuring out your serviceability.

Now that you know what banks take into account when considering your serviceability, how do you make your numbers look good?

I'll first tell you what doesn't make them look good – buying negatively-geared houses.

Many property investors accept reduced growth from purchasing these properties, as they judge their investment on their ability to provide income.

The goal of these investors is to have enough passive income to retire. That's why positive cash flow houses are their focus. They acquire properties with strong returns, and once they reach the desired cash flow, they live off their income or stop investing.

Many experts adopt this approach due to its potential to increase your serviceability. Positive cash flow makes you eligible for better loans, as banks are more confident you can repay the money.

That's the main condition for taking out a loan. Wherever your income comes from, the bank will take it into account. As a result, positive cash flow earned through properties might just be enough to qualify you for a favourable loan. This enables you to buy more houses and expand your empire.

Also, leveraging positive cash flow eliminates the risk of relying on just one strategy. For instance, if you only invest for high capital growth, you're speculating. You're forgetting your main priority – reducing mortgage debt through the tenant's income.

If you don't have a tenant or you have a tenant who doesn't pay the rent on time, you won't be able to make mortgage payments. It gets even worse if your property gets damaged since you'll need to cover expensive repairs.

This won't be a problem if your property generates positive cash flow. You'll always have some passive income to make a variety of payments. That's why I want you to adopt this strategy and not just depend on capital growth. Don't get me wrong, capital growth is also important but cash flow is the oxygen in this game and no oxygen means you're out of the game.

However, there's so much confusion in the real estate world. Investors often select the wrong approach because they're bombarded with conflicting information.

Frankly, the choice is pretty straightforward if you want to maximise your serviceability and be able to keep buying properties and grow your portfolio. Take the way businesses operate as an example.

They often want to expand by purchasing new equipment or a smaller company, but they don't have enough funds. They want to take out a loan, and the bank analyses their serviceability. If they have enough cash flow, the loan will be granted. Otherwise, they'll need to look for other sources of financing.

Cash flow is just as important to you. In a sense, running your portfolio works the same as running a company.

Additionally, positive cash flow brings you one step closer to achieving freedom and avoiding handcuffs. It prevents liability that can hinder your portfolio development and increases the chances of taking out a favourable loan.

If you don't look good in the eyes of banks, you won't have enough serviceability to stay in the game.

The only way you can keep building your portfolio is to have a steady income through positive cash flow and potential of high growth in the short and long term.

The story is different if you aim to buy just one or two properties. Cash flow is not as significant in this case. Your serviceability might be limited, and you can't move on to your next property, which is fine if this is your goal.

If you're in your 60s and you want to get decent growth out of your property, you don't need to focus on serviceability.

But if you want to create a large portfolio, serviceability is indispensable. And the only way to have it is to obtain positive cash flow.

Now, you might be wondering: "Why would I need high serviceability when I can centre my portfolio around capital growth?"

While there are numerous advocates for positive cash flow properties, there are also countless experts who deem capital growth superior.

They think real wealth can only be generated if you double your holdings every 7-10 years. According to this school of thought, investing in positive cash flow properties may not pay off in the long term.

For example, if your house is on the outskirts of a large city, these people argue your property doubles in value just once every 10-15 years. Suppose you bought the place for $500,000, and the value doubles twice in 25-30 years.

Your property should then be worth around $2 million. Although this seems highly profitable in today's terms, some people believe this won't be the case 30 years from now.

The advocates of this strategy have some great points, but should you move away from positive cash flow properties due to these arguments?

No.

Serviceability is paramount to successful real estate, and people often overlook it when buying their first property.

Therefore, you can't ignore cash flow, and you can't ignore growth, either.

In fact, you can get the best of both worlds because one doesn't preclude the other.

Any professional investor can't sustain their success without relying on both strategies.

If you only chase growth, there will be no serviceability. There will be no cash flow to secure lending.

Likewise, you'll have no long-term equity if you don't buy growth properties.

This is why both serviceability and high capital growth are vital to long-term prosperity. The only way to create wealth is to attach the growth component to your cash flow properties.

Staying in this sweet spot is much better than being a one-trick-pony investor fixated on just one strategy.

Even though there are different camps in real estate, you shouldn't join one and abandon the other. Reap the benefits of good serviceability, but don't forget about capital growth investments.

It's a Buffer Against Interest Rate Rises

You can't control many things on the market. Fluctuations happen all the time, and there's nothing you can do about them.

But this doesn't mean you can't protect your portfolio. This is critical when facing interest rate hikes.

They can directly influence your portfolio. Beyond increasing the price of the house, they can also limit capital availability and investment demand.

Furthermore, interest rate hikes can impact returns on your investments. In turn, prices change according to the inherent risk associated with real estate. The degree of these influences may not be drastic.

Nonetheless, you need to prepare for them, and the way you do that is by generating positive cash flow.

This brings us to another benefit of positive cash flow – it serves as a buffer against interest rate rises.

Many investors lose their money when interest rates go up.

Why?

Because they didn't generate enough cash flow.

If interest rates go up by just 0.5%, it can severely affect your cash flow and prevent you from buying more properties. Sometimes, you might even be forced to sell some of your houses.

But the risk is dramatically reduced if you secure enough positive cash flow. You're better prepared for interest rate rises, meaning they affect you less.

You'll probably make less money, but you'll still be able to pay down your mortgage, hold onto your properties, and ensure your portfolio remains intact.

There are many other ways to benefit from positive cash flow in terms of interest rates. To help you understand how, let's take a look at the information that determine your mortgage rates:

- Credit score
- DTI (debt-to-income) ratio
- Cash reserves
- LTV (loan-to-value) ratio on your investment property

Your finances, including your tax returns and credit report, will be analysed in more detail than when you're purchasing your home. Hence, you need a robust profile to be eligible for a favourable mortgage rate.

Positive cash flow helps you accomplish this in various ways.

First, it enables you to make a larger down payment.

This is a crucial requirement when financing your properties through conventional loans, whether your rate is fixed or adjustable.

The amounts vary, but they're usually between 15% and 25%. This is much higher compared to 2%-3% generally applied on conventional mortgages. Moreover, the down payment isn't normally eligible for discounts.

The good news is that you can make the down payment much easier if you have considerable positive cash flow. You have more passive income, allowing you to lower the interest you have to pay throughout the mortgage term.

In this case, interest rate hikes may be a setback. But the situation would be dire if you didn't have positive cash flow to repay the loan more comfortably.

Another way positive cash flow can help you with interest rates is by improving your credit score.

When you're financing properties, lenders typically look for higher credit ratings than they do with primary residence purchases.

Plus, the better your credit rating, the better terms you can secure. It falls into one of the five following categories:

- Very bad – anything below 400
- Bad – between 400 and 500
- Average – the average score is 550
- Good – between 600 and 700
- Excellent – above 700

Positive cash flow should help you land in a higher category. It can also help you repay your loans more easily, even if you don't have a good credit score.

The final reason why positive cash flow is a must-have when preparing for high interest rates is that it demonstrates your abilities as a landlord.

As you're applying for a loan to finance a rental house, the banks will look into your landlord records. If you've never managed or owned a property, it'll be much harder to get a loan.

In contrast, the fact that you have positive cash flow shows that you've proven yourself as a landlord. You're receiving passive income, which tells the bank granting the loan that you're less of a risk.

However, the lender might require you to have some reserves (a few months' worth of mortgage payments). Some banks use these funds to cover the months when there are no tenants in your house.

The final point I want you to remember is to shop around whenever interest rates rise. If you submit your loan application multiple times, you'll be more likely to get a lower rate.

Compare at least three to five banks before selecting the one that will finance your property.

Coupled with positive cash flow, this will help you cope with higher interest rates.

CHAPTER 6

Generate Your Own Capital Growth

Success in real estate can't happen if you make random choices. Inexperienced investors buy a house and pray to God that the process turns out great. That's not a good approach.

Capital growth is where the real money is made. In other words, your house needs to increase in value over time.

But the value isn't going to rise on its own. You need to make it happen.

There are four core elements that will help you generate, accelerate, and guarantee capital growth instead of waiting for it to happen. "Supply and demand" is the first one.

Supply and Demand

Supply and demand are two of the most important economic concepts, serving as the foundation of market economies. You can track many indicators in property investment in terms of supply and demand to make calculated decisions. But what exactly do these two concepts denote?

On the one hand, demand stands for how much of a service or product buyers need. This is the amount consumers want to buy at a particular price. The correlation between the quantity demanded and the price is the demand relationship.

On the other hand, supply represents the products and services the market provides. In other words, this is the quantity vendors can supply for a particular price. The correlation between goods supplied and the market is the supply relationship. Hence, the price is a reflection of supply and demand.

Another way we can explain supply and demand is to consider the law behind this correlation. This economic principle explains the interaction between the two notions and how it affects the prices of goods or services.

When the demand for a product or service is high, the price rises. By contrast, if there's a sizeable supply for an offering but the demand isn't there the price drops. The reason is simple – owners raise prices when there's a relative scarcity. But when there's an oversupply, some items will be unsold.

In fact, the housing market crash was one of the primary causes of the GFC. And the biggest reason was the law of supply and demand.

Before the crisis, consumers enjoyed relatively low interest rates. Banks provided affordable mortgages and were encouraged to relax lending standards. As a result, people who couldn't afford a house now had a fantastic opportunity to become property owners. Many customers snagged houses with minimal down payments despite having poor credit scores.

Speculative buyers also entered the market, further driving demand and cutting into supply. All of which caused prices to soar.

Supply lagged, and investors started speculating in the market to make quick money. However, the higher prices put people off buying, so they pulled out. Demand dropped, and prices followed suit. This was a prelude to the market crash and rapidly lowering property prices.

The crash demonstrates that supply and demand counteract each other. However, this doesn't go on forever – it only occurs until an equilibrium is achieved. This is the point where supply equals demand, provided all other key factors are equal.

Once the market reaches equilibrium, supply and demand achieve a balance and stabilise prices.

All this directly influences your performance in real estate. That's why you shouldn't only consider your property's location – you also need to take supply and demand into account.

Think of property like any other product or service in this regard. It moves according to changes in supply and demand.

For instance, the price rises if demand surpasses supply and vice versa. A variety of factors can explain this:

Housing Affordability

Income determines purchasing power. Therefore, it holds that rising income enables people to afford luxury purchases, like new houses. That's why the demand for homes rises during economic growth and plummets during recessions.

Speculative Demand

Higher housing demand can also be driven by high speculative demand. This concept indicates how confident buyers are about the future of particular markets. When customers expect prices to increase, housing demand rises because people want to use their wealth appropriately.

Interest Rates

Considering interest rates is paramount when making your investment decisions. If they're low, it generally leads to higher demand for properties and an uptick in prices. If they're high, demand typically plummets.

When it comes to Australia, the average interest rate stands at about 4%. It reached an all-time high (17.50%) in 1990 and plunged to a record low (0.10%) in 2020. Accordingly, consumers are more likely to borrow money when interest rates are lower, enabling them to purchase properties and thus increasing demand.

Population Growth

Population growth can also put high demand on available housing. This has been especially prevalent in Australia in the past decade. Coupled with a sharp decrease in interest rates, robust population growth led to a dramatic rise in property prices from 2012 to 2017 due to high demand.

Australia's current population is about 26 million and is expected to increase by nearly 20 million people by 2061. This would put Australia's population at approximately 46 million and cause a huge spike in housing demand.

Moreover, experts project the number of households to rise, too. Some estimates suggest it'll jump from around 9 million to approximately 13 million in 2040. Plus, there are expected to be more families by the same year. Experts anticipate the number of families to rise from around 7 million to 9.4 million.

All this promises high demand.

New Infrastructure

Building new infrastructure is a sure-fire way to drive up supply and demand in certain areas. Here are some of the projects that can achieve this effect:

- Roads, transport routes, additions to existing highways, schools, universities, hospitals, etc.
- Owners renovating their properties, which makes the area more desirable
- Private companies breaking into an area, creating more employment opportunities
- Revamped shops, cafes, facilities, and similar buildings

Mortgage Availability

Most consumers buy houses through mortgages. To obtain financing, they need to qualify for a mortgage, and the institution needs to be willing to provide it. This willingness is another major factor that influences supply and demand.

When banks grant loans, the demand rises. When banks refuse to grant loans, demand drops.

You can see why mortgage availability matters when you look at Australian figures. In 2018, a whopping 11.5% of all households spent about 30-50% of their gross income to cover mortgage costs. Another 5.5% spent at least 50%.

The reason so many people took out mortgages is that they needed housing. Hence, demand was high.

Economic Growth

Economic growth entails rising incomes, allowing consumers to buy more properties. This results in an uptick in prices and increased demand.

Although Australia took a massive hit during the COVID-19 pandemic, 2021 and 2022 have offered robust economic recovery. Property values are rising across the country and people's finances are rebounding.

Renting Cost

When looking for housing opportunities, the decision to buy or rent comes down to a simple factor – the price. If the rent is too high, more customers will try to buy because it's more cost-effective, leading to higher demand.

Now that you know how supply and demand affect property prices, you want to understand how to do proper research. These five aspects will help you determine the supply and demand in your target area:

Days on Market

The first thing you want to look at is the number of days a particular house from the target area spent being advertised before a sale. If the property takes months or even years to sell, demand is low. In contrast, homes that sell after just a few days or weeks point to high demand.

Vacancy Rate

Another numerical value you should consider is the vacancy rate. It works similarly to the vacancy rate of individual properties, showing the percentage of houses vacant at a time in the market. If the suburb is oversupplied and there's low demand, the vacancy rate will be high and vice versa.

Property Price Discounting

The final price of a property is sometimes lower than the original one due to vendor discounts. Monitoring this figure helps you assess the seller's motivation and buyer interest in the area. For example, low discounts point to strong demand. Thus, buyers don't have to provide high discounts to sell homes.

ACR and Proportion of Renters

Auction clearance rates (ACR) tell you how many auctioned properties actually sell. Suburbs with robust demand sell more properties at auctions than areas with weaker demand.

Finally, don't forget to analyse the proportion of renters. It tells you the number of tenants in a suburb. The higher the number, the stronger the demand in the area. Plus, a good mix of owners-occupiers and high rental demand is always great.

These aspects will help you determine the market you should break into, putting you on the right track to achieving capital growth. But you still have three other elements to address. The following section will delve deep into the three elements.

Population, Infrastructure, Employment – The Capital Growth Drivers to Look For

You can't have capital growth without looking at the whole picture. Besides supply and demand, you also need to consider the all-important trinity: population, infrastructure, and employment. I've mentioned them briefly in the previous section, but let's now take a closer look at their impact and the figures in Australia.

Population

One of the most important missions of every government in the world is to increase the population in their country. It provides tremendous benefits, and it particularly favours real estate investors.

Why?

Because the greater the population of a particular area, the more conducive it is to property investment. Traditionally, the national population growth rate in Australia has stood at 1-2% per year, with some high-growing areas reaching 3%.

How does it impact real estate?

Essentially, population growth leads to higher demand. It also signifies that the economy and job market are in great shape. Investing in these regions is an excellent way to boost your portfolio with valuable properties.

Australia has performed decently in terms of population growth. The number was relatively low between the 1990s and mid-2000s – compared to previous periods – due to lower immigration and declining birth rates. But Australia has enjoyed much greater population growth ever since and is projected to expand at a faster pace than 20 years ago.

Immigration is expected to be a key driver of this uptick. The government has a high-quality immigration program that makes Australia appealing to foreigners seeking excellent housing opportunities.

This especially holds for immigrants who relocate specifically to find housing. Unlike refugees or so-called urgent migrants, they can usually afford to buy a place as soon as they arrive. As a result, the higher their number, the greater the demand for properties.

There are other groups of immigrants that should spur population growth. For instance, many come to Australia for work-related reasons. They can't afford to buy a house, but they have enough money to rent. Either way, the pool of potential customers is set to expand.

The cities that receive the most immigrants include Melbourne, Sydney, and Brisbane. About 70% of all immigration takes place here, underpinning solid capital growth.

But if you break down the population moves, you can see that high capital growth also occurs at the street or suburb level. The mining boom triggered this movement in Darwin, Perth, and many other areas.

Now, when considering population growth, you shouldn't check the number of people only. The average household size is also paramount.

This is a significant component of Australia's household formation rate. It has declined since the 1950s and 1960s, meaning that the average household size has shrunk.

Various factors have been at play, such as demographic changes, responses to housing prices, and household preferences. Plus, the population has become older, and income levels have risen. All these factors shrink households.

Why is this important?

It's important because it increases the demand for housing. For instance, many people no longer want to live with their parents. Hence, they move out of the place and look for a house of their own. This has opened fantastic investment opportunities.

Infrastructure

Infrastructure projects are a pivotal contributor to capital growth. Roads, schools, shops, hospitals, and railways can make any property market more appealing to buyers, whether initiated by councils or the government.

What are the benefits of these projects?

There are numerous advantages, but the main one is the creation and support of urban renewal. Younger generations, in particular, are drawn to these areas in their search for housing. It can also lead to numerous employment opportunities to reinvigorate the economy.

As more and more people are drawn to these regions, the demand for property grows. This results in increased rents and appreciation of prices.

New infrastructure doesn't just include the construction of buildings and roads. It can also take place alongside zoning changes, allowing for high-density living. In turn, capital growth skyrockets in the short term due to higher demand for properties.

What does this mean to you as an investor?

It means you should stay on top of the changes announced by your planning department. Let's see what's taking place in certain areas of Australia.

In 2020 the Victorian government pledged about $1 billion to develop the largest flu vaccine plant in the southern hemisphere. The facility is to be constructed near Melbourne Airport, promoting massive capital growth in the region. They've also earmarked more than $2 billion to build new stops and tunnels to enhance rail travel in various metro areas.

More states are investing in infrastructure and not just Victoria. NSW has allocated a whopping $72 billion for improvements in roads and rail, which should lead to massive demand.

And the risk of failed investments is virtually non-existent. Don't forget that an enormous amount of COVID stimulus is circulating in the country. The interest rates are also low, allowing people to borrow more money and buy houses.

Buying properties near these regions is a smart choice. Recent lifestyle changes can also help you make your decision.

For instance, the pandemic has shown that many people want to live near green spaces with high mobility and easy access to amenities. These improvements help them lead a better life, meaning they're more likely to buy properties in the vicinity.

You need to seize these opportunities to accomplish impressive capital growth.

Employment

The final part of the trinity is employment. It plays a critical role in creating and accelerating capital growth for property investors for a simple reason.

If the employment rate is high, the population is more likely to support price growth in certain areas and pay rent. On the other hand, if a large portion of the population is unemployed, it negatively affects property performance because people can't afford to buy or rent a place.

Job growth is generally attributed to employers and employees who enjoy rising economic opportunities. Several markets have expanded in the past two years, including retail and real estate. They've opened numerous opportunities all over the country, creating thousands of jobs for Australians.

On the international level, Australia has a relatively low unemployment rate, sitting at approximately 5%. It can be higher in smaller markets that rely on limited commerce and industries like lower socio-economic regions and mining towns. But other areas enjoy high employment.

So, when there are fewer unemployed people, the markets rise. The real estate market is the one that especially benefits from this trend.

Many Australians want to stop paying rent and buy a place of their own. The majority of them have a steady source of income that creates the opportunity for them to purchase a house, be it through loans or using all their own funds. Low interest rates are another incentive, so people want to grab these opportunities while they still exist.

Healthy employment rates also have a significant impact on supply and demand. With more jobs filled, individuals can buy more properties, ensuring robust demand. This demand is met with adequate supply from property investment firms and owners who want to sell their properties.

But selling is just one way to make the most of high job-growth areas. As previously mentioned, not everyone is interested in buying. Many individuals can't take out loans, so they rent properties. This demand leads to lower vacancy rates, which helps you yield lofty profits.

In 2022, Australia has increased the labour force to nearly 14 million people. A range of industries have been at the forefront of this trend.

For example, the population is aging and continuing to grow. This means there are more children and elderly in the country, raising the demand for healthcare services. Targeting areas with these facilities is an excellent decision.

Another sector that's boosted job growth is infrastructure. As discussed earlier, the population is on the rise and moving into many major cities in Australia. This has driven the demand for several projects, like hotels, hospitals, entertainment facilities, apartment complexes, and houses. Plus, the construction industry is expected to grow by approximately 11% in the next 3-5 years, creating jobs and facilitating capital growth.

Finally, teaching has become an essential career. Australians are eager to shape the minds of future generations, leading to high demand in this industry. Supported by a growing population, this sector is set to rise by about 12% in the upcoming period. Again, you can score a major profit if you invest in properties near high-quality educational institutions.

This trinity (population, infrastructure, and employment) should be at the top of your list of priorities when looking for investment opportunities. If you have two of them, the third will happen naturally.

If you have the infrastructure, people will move to the region to find jobs.

If you have people and employment, the government will start building the infrastructure around it.

And once all three are in play, property prices appreciate, and capital growth happens.

Achieving True Wealth

Properties with high capital growth let you accomplish phenomenal results. You can build a sizeable portfolio with valuable houses. But what can you do to take your real estate game to the next level?

You focus on cash flow to achieve true wealth.

This may run against what you constantly hear about real estate. Many people believe that the only way to retire is to create a portfolio and withdraw a small amount per year (3-4%). This way, they won't run out of money.

So, what's the main problem with this strategy?

It's simple – most people can hardly replace their lifestyle by withdrawing only a limited amount of money. Furthermore, they depend on the stability of the financial system to keep their funds unaffected. But as we've seen countless times, disasters lurk behind every corner and can cripple your assets.

To avoid this situation, your best strategy is to invest in cash flow properties. As you approach retirement, cash flow is a critical piece of the puzzle. Unlike fixed-income investments, they have high yields and are less volatile.

Let's take a look at two investing scenarios to demonstrate the benefits of having ample cash flow.

Suppose your neighbour is a budding investor. He had been slaving away for decades at a workplace that was far from his dream job. Throughout his career, he put away money to provide for the family and their future. Before he retired, he received several raises, and his final annual salary was $150,000.

This was a considerable amount of money, but it wasn't enough to secure his family's future. He took up property investment and achieved excellent results. His net worth grew to around $2 million, and he is finally ready to retire.

However, he's still not sure whether the funds will last. He turns to his financial advisor, who tells him he can withdraw approximately 3-4% per year to stay safe.

His pre-tax cash flow is $60,000, which is a lot of money, and his expenses should be lower after he retires. But keep in mind that he made $150K per year before his retirement, so he needs to change his lifestyle drastically.

On top of that, a large part of his investment portfolio lies in stocks. These aren't hard assets, making them highly volatile. A market crash can lead to a major loss.

So, did your neighbour plan his retirement correctly? Not by any stretch of the imagination. It'll be hard, if not impossible, to get used to a downgraded lifestyle. Additionally, taxes will reduce his income even further, and his stock investments will destabilise his overall portfolio.

Now let's take a look at another investor. She's still young, having only been employed for about 10 years. Her career has been successful, allowing her to rake in $80K a year. Still, she's not happy with her financial performance and wants to maximise her earning power.

Rather than solely focusing on her career, she's purchased properties that generate high cash flow. She's bought several single-family houses and is a passive investor in several properties. These moves have earned her a 10% annual return.

Now, let's assume she has a similar career to your neighbour, building $2 million in net worth and raising her salary to $150K. But instead of compromising her future with mindless stock investment, she decides to go against the tide.

She continues to develop her portfolio with different types of property. The annual cash flow on the same investment is about $200,000, which is well over her final salary. What's more, all her investment comes down to hard assets, making her finances less volatile. In turn, she doesn't need to worry about her future as much as your neighbour.

She won't need to change her lifestyle, either. In fact, she can improve it significantly since her income is now much higher.

What about her retirement plans? Let me remind you that this investor is much younger than your neighbour. She's still in her 30s and doesn't have to toil away for another 20 years in a business she doesn't like. Travelling the world is a much better option, and the $200,000 in cash flow lets her do that easily.

But let's assume that her net worth is much lower and not $2 million. She's happy living on $60K a year like the first investor. At her 10% return, she would need $600,000 to achieve her goal. Naturally, it's much quicker to earn $600K than $2 million.

You might think this isn't nearly enough to retire, but that's beside the point. She can retire if she decides to do so since she has a lot of passive income ($200,000 per year). This gives her financial independence.

And more importantly, it allows her to create true wealth because she can afford more properties. Even if some of them don't perform as desired, it won't take a massive toll on her finances. Her cash flow serves as a safety net.

Another thing you need to consider is the tax. Unlike the first investor, this lady focused on real estate only, giving her direct ownership. As a result, tremendous tax benefits will be coming her way, such as capital gains and depreciation. This allows her to hold onto a larger portion of her income.

In addition, the borrowing power of the second investor is much greater. If she wants to take out a loan to finance more purchases, she'll be able to do so more easily. Lenders are impressed by her financial situation. Her credit is high, her assets are terrific, but most importantly – she has a sizeable passive income.

Plus, she can submit her portfolio as evidence. Once banks see her properties generate positive cash flow, they'll consider her a talented investor. Therefore, granting her funds is not as risky as granting them to the first investor.

These examples demonstrate that cash flow is the best strategy for expanding your empire and building wealth. The extra money earned through passive income helps you pay off the mortgage of your properties. It also lets you save for additional down payments to finance more houses sooner.

The more cash flow your portfolio generates, the more money you can save. Ultimately, you'll be able to accomplish your property investment goals faster.

The Short Term Is Always Tougher

Capital growth is a phenomenal long-term strategy. It ties especially well into my advice that you should only buy properties with land. If you buy houses with no land or apartment units, you won't have control of the place, and there will be no or little appreciation.

Unfortunately, you can't do anything with those types of properties. The story changes if you buy a place with big land. In this case, both the home and the lot increase in value, resulting in high profits.

Calculating capital growth is instrumental in assessing property performance when making decisions. It serves as a litmus test for comparing different houses with similar variables, such as interest rates, expenses, and financing margin.

Even if you're not assessing properties, calculating capital growth lets you decide if investing in a house is worth it in the first place. All you need to do is compare capital growth to Australia's interest rate. If the projected growth is higher, your investment should pay off.

Here's a quick example to illustrate this.

Say you're planning on purchasing a house with a lot of land using your fixed deposit account, which generally delivers returns of 3-4% per year. If the calculated capital growth is 5%, you can invest in the place safely. But if it's less than 3%, you might want to choose a different property.

This in-depth analysis lets you structure your portfolio more effectively, which is especially important when buying your first house. You'll want to expand a few months down the line to ensure a higher income to provide for your family and retire easily. Thus, you want to know the resale potential of the place and if it can deliver a hefty profit after a particular period.

Calculating capital growth allows you to do just that by rearranging the current and future values. For instance, suppose you have a target selling price for your first house. You expect a 5% return per year according to past trends and similar places in the area. By computing growth, you can figure out how much time it'll take before you meet your goal.

But keep in mind that achieving remarkable capital growth takes a lot of time. If you don't have enough cash to support your outgoings in the meantime, your investment will miss the mark.

So, how do you survive until your properties deliver capital growth? You invest in positive cash flow houses.

We've covered several metrics you need to analyse to identify positive cash flow properties. For example, you should consider the vacancy rate. Ideally, you should look for places with a vacancy rate under 2%. Some of my clients are even more successful, as they frequently buy houses with a 0.5% vacancy rate or less.

What does this tell you?

It tells you that there's a huge rental demand for houses, offering great opportunities to score high rent and potentially capital growth. But I can't stress this enough – they need to deliver positive cash flow.

As indicated earlier, you need to look at your portfolio as a business. And cash flow is imperative in any business. If you don't have enough of it, your company shuts down.

The same thing happens in real estate. If you don't have sufficient cash flow, you'll run out of money and may never reach high capital growth. Your portfolio will extinguish way before that.

Consequently, achieving financial independence is impossible. You strive for freedom, but at the same time you're buying a handcuff if you purchase negatively geared properties.

Another reason cash flow is essential is that it lets you stay in the property game. After all, you can only make headway if you leverage the bank money. But the lenders won't give you money if your income isn't going up. Cash flow increases your earnings, making your finances more favourable in the eyes of banks.

Now, you don't need to worry about propping up your capital growth with cash flow if your goal is to buy one or two properties. This is a great way to supplement your monthly income, but will it help you build a steady portfolio and retire?

No.

The only way to do that is to play the investment game properly by ensuring cash flow. Not only does it bolster your finances, but it also improves your mindset. You see money entering your pockets, which alleviates stress. You're motivated to do more deals and set the stage for capital growth.

If both ingredients are in place (cash flow and capital growth), you won't run out of serviceability. You'll be able to sustain your operations, enabling you to create a stable financial future.

And the best part is that you don't need colossal capital growth to keep going. For instance, suppose you bought a house for $1 million with a 5% annual capital growth. This gives you $50,000 per year from just one property.

After a certain period, you can sell the house for a solid profit and pay off your mortgage. What does this give you? It gives you even more cash flow.

This way, you can utilise your serviceability to take your portfolio to a whole new level. The trick is to stay consistent and stay true to your original tactics – making sure your houses are in high-growth locations. This guarantees their value goes up.

Luckily, finding these properties is relatively simple in today's market. Australian supply is steady, as the infrastructure projects have picked up in the last two years. New buildings are popping up nearly every week in major cities, so the supply is there. Demand is also quite high because the population is growing, and there are many new jobs.

You can capitalise on these opportunities with sound investment strategies. And positive cash flow should be at the core, as it paves the way for capital growth.

CHAPTER 7

Four Value-Add Strategies to Supercharge Your Portfolio

The best thing about real estate is that there are countless methods to make money. However, some strategies outperform others.

For example, so-called turnkey properties might seem like an excellent option. These places require little-to-no work on your part. However, the main problem with this tactic is its low potential. You can only make a limited amount of money, as you're adding no extra value to the house for a while.

This brings me to a superior approach – the value-add method.

Value-add investing involves active strategies that create more value in your real estate investments through making smaller changes to the property, development, or renovation. This method normally focuses on buying established properties.

Through hands-on management, you work to increase your property's market value, income potential and seek enhanced returns.

You should stick to individual houses with land because this lets you make the most of the value-add approach. They require additional capital depending upon the value add, but the capital growth potential is much higher. They're not restricted by various management laws, offering more flexibility in terms of making enhancements and changes.

On top of that, houses on larger parcels may attract tenants who rent longer. And if they're in a high-growth area, your capital growth can reach extraordinary levels.

The reason they're called value-add properties is that they require corrective action to fulfil potential value. An array of troubles may have taken place and lowered their value, such as deferred maintenance, low lease rates, substandard facilities, and below-market occupancy.

To generate a solid ROI with these places, you need to put in capital and some effort. Some of the best ways to get a property market-ready and boost its value are renovations, restructuring, and changing the way it delivers income.

These repositioning efforts make the premises more appealing to tenants due to a variety of capital improvements.

Keep in mind that you can't execute this strategy correctly without the appropriate tools. You need to understand the condition of your house. You also need to perform comprehensive market analyses, as most of the factors pertaining to valuation take place on the market. Plus, generating and maintaining a high cash flow is a huge plus.

The most significant advantage of value-add property investment is the potential to boost ROI. You can find diamonds in the rough, use your equity, and make appropriate changes to sell the property or hold onto it for cash flow. This way, you maximise your profit.

Another great thing about the approach is that it comes with all benefits associated with commercial purchases. Besides long-term positive cash flow, you can also enjoy high appreciation.

We've covered the basics of value-adding. Now let's see the four core strategies of this tactic.

The first strategy is cosmetic renovations. This is a highly recommended method for adding tons of value.

For example, it's perfect for houses with, say, an outdated kitchen or peeling paint. You can quickly increase the value of this place by making simple improvements. This gives you manufactured equity and enables you to bump up the rent.

In the worst-case scenario, the manufactured equity will be the same as your investment, so there will be no loss. However, this happens rarely.

You're much more likely to generate between two to three times more than your investment through cosmetic revamps. As a result, there's instant profit, and you've yet to even consider the rent increase you're now entitled to.

The second strategy is adding a granny flat. Different rules dictate this purchase, meaning some Australian regions are better suited for this method than others. NSW for example, is ideal for granny flats since the potential for manufactured equity is enormous.

I regularly invest in granny flats, and the results are amazing. For example, I generated $10,000 additional income from one of my investment properties by building a granny flat.

However, I did my research beforehand, and you need to do the same. Check the rules around this strategy because some states have strict rules about who can live in granny flats.

The next effective tactic is to find houses with a floor plan. For instance, some of your properties might have three bedrooms, and you may want to add another one. Consider the arrangement of the place to find the solution. If it has two living rooms, you can convert one of them into a bedroom, which requires minimal changes and may cost around $5,000.

Your property now goes from a three-bedroom house to four. And suddenly you have increased the value of the property by at least 8%, and all you had to do was make a minimal investment and alteration.

The results can be just as impressive if you rent the place out. Many tenants appreciate houses with more bedrooms, allowing you to set a higher price tag.

The final value-add strategy you need to try is subdivision. While it requires some skill, experience, and a land surveyor, it's one of the most effective ways to maximise your profits. It boils down to purchasing a property with a large lot of land you can subdivide. This way, you can build another house or if possible, sell the land for an instant financial boost.

What investors like about these four methods most is that they can be combined. You can buy a house, add a granny flat, renovate it, subdivide it, and incorporate another bedroom. This gives you much more manufactured equity, generating high cash flow, and allowing you to buy more properties.

It's also how I've managed to build my portfolio in a short period. You can have the same results too, if not even better.

The key is to apply the four strategies appropriately, and I'll explain how to do so in the following sections.

Granny Flat

A granny flat is generally defined as a secondary dwelling. This property usually shares the same lot as the primary dwelling. They're also self-contained, meaning they come with a separate entrance, bathroom, bedroom, living space, kitchen, and laundry room.

This modest structure is a fantastic way to expand a property. For instance, many people have teenagers who need more space while retaining the perks of living with their parents. Alternatively, their elderly dad or mum might be looking for a neat little place where they can spend more time with their grandchildren.

But it's also exceedingly popular in the investment world, allowing you to generate high rental income. Granny flats are also incredibly flexible and provide you with tons of benefits.

First, building one is a cheap way to become a property investment owner. If you're not ready to purchase a larger house as your first investment, you can begin by building a granny flat.

Second, these units let you make a lot of extra money through rent. Depending on its location, you can easily earn about $300-$500 per week, enabling you to cover your mortgage or other costs.

Another great part about being a granny flat owner is that you can easily maintain your unit. It's right next to your main dwelling and it's smaller, so looking after the property isn't time-consuming.

Finally, these dwellings can skyrocket your property's value, especially if it abides by the local laws. This means you can sell the place at a higher price, as more people are attracted to your well-maintained flat.

While granny flats are flexible, this doesn't mean you can rent out or sell just any unit. You'll need to consider several crucial details:

- Privacy and safety of the tenants – Granny flats must have separate pathways and entrances to provide the tenants with easy access to their abode.

- Attractive location – If you want to make the most of your granny flat investment, make sure the primary dwelling is in a popular suburb with various amenities. Granny flats with nearby hospitals, offices, and shopping centres can be a real cash cow.

- Design – You want to design your granny flats to look the same as your principal residence. In other words, people need to be comfortable living on the premises. Therefore, leave plenty of room for the tenants to add personal touches, like painting the walls in a neutral colour.

- Do thorough research – Before adding the flat to a property, determine if it's a profitable investment. Consider the regulations, the demand in the area, and the expenses associated with the project. Your best bet is to obtain accurate quotes from various contractors and builders to get a clear idea of the price tag.

- Don't go overboard – A granny flat is supposed to be relatively small. It shouldn't take up a large outdoor space or dominate the garden.

When it comes to the cost of building granny flats, it can vary considerably, depending on several factors. Primarily, the type of the premise and location play a pivotal role in the total expenses. But in general, you can expect a ballpark figure of about $100K to $200K to get the residence fully functional.

There are several types and designs you can go for, such as modular and prefabricated homes and dwellings built from scratch. Some of the things that may influence your choice are the budget, available designs, and features you wish to incorporate into the abode.

If you plan to add the granny flat as part of your extension or renovation projects, the price could even exceed $200,000. You also need to take into account the architect's fees, engineering costs, and money going into potential or existing hazards (e.g., asbestos).

Regarding financing, there are also a variety of options. Two of the most common solutions are to use your home's equity or take out another mortgage. However, you should first consider having your dwelling revalued.

As previously mentioned, you're free to choose how you want to add the granny flat to the property. You can incorporate a standalone unit in the yard or extend the garage. Nevertheless, don't forget that the structure needs to meet certain regulations, which vary by state.

For instance, getting a granny flat in NSW requires you to obtain the green light from a licensed accreditor. Otherwise, you risk being fined. As for renting in this state, you can rent the dwelling out to anyone, including unrelated parties.

Other states that are conducive to profitable granny flat investments are Western Australia, Australian Capital Territory, Tasmania, Northern Territory and Queensland. You can easily use this type of dwelling to supplement your income through rent.

In contrast, getting approval for granny flats is hard in Victoria, especially if you want to rent the place out. Some areas don't allow you to earn income through the dwelling. Therefore, you can build the unit, but only if dependent individuals live in it. The state may also permit you to use the premises as your home office, additional living room, or personal studio.

Similar restrictions apply in South Australia. Renting out granny flats in these states may incur hefty fines. But make sure to check with your local council in case the regulations change. I believe granny flats are the best way to make the housing affordable and it's a win-win for both renters and investors.

The final thing to keep in mind is tax deductions. Once you rent out your granny flat for extra income, you'll be subject to taxes on the income earned. The amount depends on your marginal rate and tax bracket.

The deductions you're eligible for depend on whether the unit is negatively or positively geared. If your rental income doesn't cover the maintenance costs (loan payments and other expenses), your dwelling is negatively geared, preventing you from claiming tax deductions. But if you own a positively geared granny flat, you should be able to obtain maintenance costs as sizeable tax deductions.

In addition to maintenance costs, you may also be entitled to tax deductions in the form of value depreciation each year. Just remember that capital gains tax (CGT) liability typically applies to the part of the property rented out and not the entire property.

Renovation

If you don't mind getting your hands dirty, investing in places that need renovations can be a highly fruitful tactic. The principle is straightforward: you buy a property in need of a revamp, make appropriate value-add changes, and sell for a profit or even better rent it out and hold it for a longer term.

Done strategically, this method can skyrocket your income. Plus, it can make your portfolio much more valuable, enabling you to accomplish your goals rapidly.

This approach requires careful planning, but that's not what you may have concluded from prime-time reality TV shows. They usually present a glorified idea of renovations. A team buys a shabby hotel and invests thousands of dollars for a revamp to sell the place for extraordinary profits.

They make it seem glamorous and effortless. However, this rarely happens.

You don't make money in real estate by purchasing a place, renovating, and flipping it. After interest, holding costs, selling commissions, tax, and stamp duty, this strategy yields barely any profit.

Conversely, buying, renovating, refinancing, and holding the property for a certain period is a time-tested approach that works much better. It perfectly ties into my point about capital growth – instead of selling the place immediately, you ensure your property appreciates over time.

Think about it. Why would you get rid of something that you put so much effort into and sacrifice your profits? The expenses are too high, keeping you from making a decent amount of money.

You're much better off holding onto the place and leveraging time to realise its wealth potential. If you renovate your place and retain it, you can expect tremendous gains:

- High manufactured equity and accelerated capital growth
- The rental property is more appealing to a larger number of tenants, allowing you to rent the place out for more money
- Tax benefits in the form of depreciation allowances

With the right determination and tools, you can find perfect opportunities to invest and renovate houses in nearly any location. Ideally, the dwelling should be at least 20-30% under the median price in the area. It should also be cosmetically distressed and poorly presented.

For instance, you can target houses with low curb appeal, peeling paintwork, poor landscaping, an unattractive exterior, or an outdated interior but with an excellent foundation. These properties don't look great, but their potential is high. Many tenants find them stunning with just a few cosmetic touches.

That said, there are also some properties you want to avoid. Look for the following warning signs:

- Bad foundation and roof – If the house doesn't appear to be in terrible shape, but it's been vacated for a while, several issues could be at play. Have the foundation and roof checked by professionals to rule out structural problems, as they're sometimes invisible from the outside. An expert can look for cracks in walls or parts of the roof caused by foundation shifts or other scenarios.

- Plumbing and electrical problems – Fixing these may require you to fork over a lot of money, potentially ruining your chance of profiting from the property. Be sure to hire seasoned inspectors to check the systems.

- Rotten boards – Another issue you might not be able to uncover is rotten boards because paint usually covers them. Again, book a technician to examine the doors and windows to ensure no boards are rotted.

Once you find the perfect property, it's time to start the renovations. Here are a few tips that will help you revamp your house correctly:

Focus on Cosmetic Improvements

Your main goal when fixing a property is to get it ready for a tenant, or maybe a sale, depending upon your strategy. As mentioned earlier, you don't want to be stuck with a place that requires major structural changes.

Besides, tenants and buyers pay more for the visible things, not foundations and electrical lines. They don't care if you spend your money re-roofing and rewiring the place.

People are now more discerning and have higher expectations. Dishwashers and TVs used to be luxury items, but they're a must nowadays. This especially applies to inner-city suburbs that appeal to affluent renters and purchasers.

That's why you want to get the biggest bang for your buck and avoid major structural changes. They don't add tangible value despite requiring a ton of money.

Instead, focus on cosmetic improvements, such as window furnishings, light fixtures, and upgrading the floors. You can also consider replacing or updating the bathroom or kitchen. Other options include installing high-quality appliances, painting the walls in neutral colours, or repairing smaller issues, like cracks on doors or torn carpets.

This way, you'll dramatically boost the value of the property while minimising the costs, which brings me to my next tip:

Stick to Your Budget

Before you purchase a house that needs renovations, schedule a professional assessment. Have the building thoroughly examined to figure out how much work needs to be done.

The key here is to get quotes from several contractors, and not just one. This will ensure you can bring the place up to modern standards for a reasonable price.

From there, you shouldn't have issues drawing up your budget and getting an overall picture of the outlay when the place is rent-ready. Consider all costs, including the holding expenses during the revamp period when you'll have to make interest repayments without the help of occupants. Furthermore, draw up a contingency plan – what happens if you exceed 10-15% of the budget due to unforeseen costs?

Don't Get Caught Up in the Project

One of the best things about renovations is that they can be enjoyable. While you may have fun revamping the place, don't get caught up in the project. You may lose sight of your end goal, which is to make money.

My previous tip should help you focus. Make the property presentable while following your budget.

It'll be tempting to spend more money on a dream kitchen but remember – this isn't your dream. Your goal is to satisfy demand, not your tastes.

Also, don't forget there's bound to be some renovation damage when the house receives tenants. You might need to replace drapes or carpets just a few months into their tenancy. Therefore, don't buy the most expensive items. Go for attractive products without overspending.

Subdivision

Another method of adding value to your properties is through subdivisions. I've used this strategy multiple times, as you've learned from my journey.

For example, one of my most profitable subdivisions was part of a joint venture. My Joint Venture partner sold his part for a great profit, but I didn't want to pull the trigger just yet. Instead, I built a house with a granny flat on my parcel of land, generating $14,000 in positive cash flow.

This wouldn't have been possible if my Joint Venture partner and I hadn't subdivided the property. The place would have been much more expensive and jeopardised my profits. Thankfully, the subdivision came through.

The process is relatively straightforward but requires greater understanding of council town planning rules and regulations. It involves the conversion of a parcel into two or more blocks, but the scale can vary drastically. For instance, you might be converting rural zoned blocks into residential lots or splitting a developed lot into two. These examples differ greatly, but each involves a lengthy legal procedure and carries crucial feasibility considerations.

One of the best things about subdivisions is that they can be done on different types of properties. Contrary to popular belief, you don't need to buy a huge lot of land to develop multiple allotments. Many experienced investors opt for a smaller suburban block if it adheres to the planning guidelines.

Consequently, they can capitalise on the land value while maintaining the property as a steady source of positive cash flow. That's why you want to purchase houses in areas that allow for quick subdivision approvals, and the demand for property is high.

Many locations enable you to subdivide existing properties to achieve tremendous uplift and capital growth. This simple yet effective strategy usually delivers enough equity to finance future investments.

Some people leverage larger blocks of land to maximise long-term potential. They either subdivide the land and sell a parcel or build another property on the new lot to increase their portfolio. Nonetheless, it's an excellent way to improve your serviceability and support capital growth.

Another reason you should practice subdivisions is that they typically require little effort. The most demanding part is to apply for the approval (which I'll get to shortly). Other than that, you need to ensure the place has access to essential infrastructure like electricity, sewer lines, and water.

Of course, building houses on the subdivided land complicates the endeavour due to additional considerations. These include planning, construction, hiring contractors, site managers, builders, and obtaining permits.

Now that we've covered the basics of subdivisions, let's see what the process looks like step-by-step:

Getting Educated

What's the point of buying a property with subdivision potential if there's no way to develop the property? Informing yourself beforehand prevents this risk.

Due diligence regarding subdivisions involves investigating all details relevant to your property:

- Zoning
- Previous development permits
- Market activity
- Bushfire/Flood area
- Soil contamination

- Minimum lot size

All these can influence the value of your house and land plus there are various other factors to consider especially when looking for subdivision sites. If some of these elements don't look good, you might not be able to execute the subdivision. But where do you obtain the necessary information?

Primarily, you want to consult the local council. You might be able to access the records of their meetings or environmental plans to figure out what it takes to apply for a permit. Plus, you can determine the minimum lot size in your area and go through previous approvals to ensure you're not violating any guidelines.

Due diligence consists of many other aspects:

- Enquiring with the local council to find out how long development applications take on average. This can vary by project and council, but you'll need a ballpark number to organise yourself.

- Investigating if you can connect extra services to your block. Are the water and sewage lines easy to link, or do you need to talk to neighbouring properties? That's where a local town planner who understands the local council rules and land surveyor can be very handy to have on your team while working on such projects.

- Consulting sales data and listings to determine if demand for vacant blocks or new properties is high. This will let you know if all the time and effort spent applying for the subdivision, developing infrastructure, and constructing new properties will pay off. Accordingly, you can establish a feasibility study to support your plan. It outlines your project in detail, with all goals, projected profits, and timeframes.

- Covering all costs. You can include this in your feasibility study to provide an overview of various expenses, such as stamp duty, application, legal fees, and surveyor fees. This is the only way to gauge if the subdivision is worth implementing, and it also tells you how high a budget you need.

- Verifying the location isn't subject to restrictions due to the owner's financial situation. The property's certificate of title should contain this information.

Purchase the Property

If everything about the property and subdivision potential checks out, the next step is to buy it. Use your preferred financing (e.g., loan, equity or cash) to continue the project.

Apply

Being the owner of the property, you can submit your subdivision application to the local council or use a private town planner or architect to submit the same. Keep track of it regularly by contacting staff members to determine the progress. This way, you can react on time if something goes wrong during the administration.

Furthermore, stay calm during the process and ask if you can offer assistance to speed it up. Good councils work fast and want to be efficient, so they may accept your proposal.

Act on the Permit

Once the council gives you the green light, start the subdivision process and other necessary work. You should be able to provide water and electricity without any restrictions at this point. The same goes for the construction of any new dwellings on the land.

Obtain Final Confirmation

After completing all projects, the local council will need to inspect your property to verify it abides by the plans. The assessment differs by territory and state.

Once the inspection checks out, your new block will be registered under the appropriate title. You can now rent the place or add more value to raise your profits.

New Build

A large part of being a property investor is weighing things up. For example, you often need to decide to invest in new buildings or renovations. Both strategies have their pros and cons.

On the one hand, the most significant advantage of new construction might be depreciation. All fittings and fixtures will be brand new, making you entitled to depreciation benefits. If your property is positively geared, you can save on taxes by claiming the depreciation against your income.

Another great thing about new buildings is that you can choose the most suitable design for the market. In other words, you can make it as attractive as possible to your ideal tenants or buyers. Analyse their needs and make sure the new structure accommodates them.

For example, if you're targeting large families, your property will need at least three or four bedrooms and two bathrooms. This increases the value of the place and reduces the time it spends advertised for sale.

Moreover, investing in new properties is highly recommended because it can deliver instant equity. If you buy smart and you know what you're doing, you can buy land and build a home for a relatively low cost. This maximises your profits.

Building from scratch can be a profitable strategy, but this doesn't mean it's perfect. On the contrary, there are several things you need to consider before implementing it.

First, new properties are sometimes overpriced for their market. You build a place from scratch and include all fittings to appeal to your tenants or buyers. But as previously discussed, you might get carried away during the process and buy the most expensive furniture or other additions.

While the house may be valuable, it can also be overpriced for the market. Your target clients might not be able to afford it. As a result, you're forced to settle for much lower profits or suffer a loss.

Another disadvantage of investing in new properties is that they provide no income while you're constructing them. Many people overlook this, but building a house takes months or years, depending on your project. It may not seem like a huge issue, but don't forget – a developing property generates no income.

As you're building the place, you need to cover your mortgage and make other payments. This is the main reason people abandon their projects midway through construction. They can't afford so much pressure on their finances.

The only way you can make it to the end of the building phase is to have enough cash flow. The income generated through other properties must be high enough to keep you afloat until the project is finished.

Now let's move on to renovating existing properties. I've mentioned many reasons why this strategy adds value to your property, but what else makes this method advantageous?

For starters, there's tremendous potential to buy existing properties below market value. There are deals all over the country – the key is to do your research and compare properties from individual areas. If a house sells for a lower price than other homes in the neighbourhood, make sure to snag it before your competition.

Additionally, existing properties are usually land locked. Accessing them may be trickier, but these houses are in established areas. This means that it's doubtful that new homes will be built in the vicinity and disrupt supply and demand.

Another thing investors like about existing properties is that they're more predictable than new builds. Even before buying these dwellings, you typically already know what you can rent them out for. Plus, you can find a tenant as soon as you become the owner by advertising the place beforehand. This provides you with predictable, instant income.

As for the negative, the biggest one associated with renovating existing houses is the expense. Unlike places built from scratch, these properties aren't brand-new. There might be several rooms you need to revamp if the home is dilapidated or you'll need to address faulty systems such as plumbing and electricity. They deteriorate over time, and you'll hardly be able to rent out the dwelling unless you take care of the issues.

You also have less freedom when purchasing houses for renovations, as you can't design the place your way. You can repaint them or change the furniture, but the layout remains the same. This can be a problem in terms of attracting your ideal customers.

Lastly, existing properties often have hidden problems that can prevent you from profiting if you don't do your due diligence. There might be issues with the roof, foundation, dry rot, or mould. All these are expensive to fix and can put off potential tenants. Therefore, you should always schedule inspection services before purchasing these places to determine if you can afford to address these problems.

Building a house from scratch and renovating a dwelling can add a ton of value to your portfolio. However, the projects require careful planning, effort, and money. You need to ensure the undertaking fits your budget to avoid unpleasant surprises down the line.

If you opt for new builds, here are the things you'll need to consider:

- Do you have enough time to manage tradesmen and builders?
- Do your finances allow you to build a home from scratch?
- Will the local council approve your plans?
- Are there any building restrictions you should be aware of?
- How should you design the place to attract the most people?

Likewise, you can't renovate a dwelling unless you've done your research. Ask yourself these questions to ensure you're ready for the project:

- Do I have enough time to monitor the renovations?

- Is it cheaper to renovate the place or build a property from scratch?
- Does the property have any heritage listings or other restrictions?
- Will the council approve my proposal?
- Have I addressed any hidden problems?
- Does the layout of the house allow me to rent out or sell the place to my ideal customers?

CHAPTER 8

Buying Under Value to Accelerate Your Wealth

Nowshad and Touhida are a couple from Bangladesh who've recently started their investment journey. They wanted to reinvigorate their lifestyle and avoid being heavily reliant on their career. They looked for a better financial future, so they turned to me.

One of the things I like about this hard-working couple is their background. Namely, Nowshad works in a bank, approving mortgages. Therefore, he understands how finances work, which is a huge plus in real estate.

Nowshad and Touhida had a residence in Sydney. The motivation was there, but they needed a partner to point them in the right direction. With my help, they purchased three remarkable properties in just five months.

The first house they bought was a place with a 643-square metre lot in regional QLD. They purchased the property for $328,000. They're renting the dwelling out for a fantastic $400 per week, delivering a little more than $4,000 in positive cash flow annually. On top of that, they achieved 9.7% capital growth in five months, translating into $32,000 of additional value.

This was an excellent buy. It inspired Nowshad and Touhida to look for more high-yielding properties.

They found another one in a similar place (regional QLD) just three months later. The price of this property was slightly lower than the first one ($313,500), but the parcel was larger (655 square metres).

This proved an even better purchase. Nowshad and Touhida are renting it out for $430 per week, generating nearly $4,500 in positive cash flow every year. Moreover, the capital growth on this abode was $36,500 or 11.6% in three months.

Another great thing about this place is that it was bought off the market. As a result, there was virtually no competition, allowing the couple to purchase the house for less money.

The third house Nowshad and Touhida bought was also a great decision. This property was purchased off the market for $380,000, and they rented it out for $410 per week. It earns them $3,328 in cash flow per year, and the current value of the place is $400,000. This means they achieved a 5% capital growth in just 30 days.

Many beginner investors have a hard time buying one high-profit property. Nowshad and Touhida have now purchased three phenomenal houses.

The end results are impressive. They're now earning $11,804 of positive cash flow annually and have achieved $88,500 in capital growth. After 7 months, the couple bought their fourth investment property for $500,000 which is renting for $550 per week and had capital growth of 14% in the next 9 months. You can see how this couple bought four investment properties in a matter of one year.

The main reason behind their success is that they've relied on savvy strategies. They looked for positively geared properties in high capital growth areas. Furthermore, the vacancy rates were low, enabling Nowshad and Touhida to rent them out relatively quickly.

However, that's not all. The couple also purchased three properties off the market. These houses were undervalued, paving the way for higher returns.

Now that I've given examples of buying under value, I'll explain the advantages of the strategy and how to identify these properties.

Buying Below Replacement Cost

Nowshad and Touhida used several strategies to buy below market value. Purchasing below replacement costs was one of them. The replacement cost is the price you need to cover to replace your existing property with another one.

This is a staple of value-oriented property investing. It rests on the belief that houses have underlying intrinsic values you can determine through evaluation and analysis. If the purchase price of a dwelling is lower than the intrinsic value, you can make highly profitable investments. The replacement cost method helps you do so.

Figuring out the replacement cost is generally used for new developments. It provides guidelines for an existing project and is generally more useful than capitalisation rates.

Determining the replacement cost of a property requires you to gather several construction-related estimates:

- Soft costs (fees, permits, and third-party consultants)
- Hard costs (driveway, building, site)
- Unforeseen costs
- Developer profit and construction fees
- Leasing and marketing costs
- Financing costs

When calculating the replacement cost, most people calculate the price per square metre. For instance, replacing a property in Victoria may be more expensive than performing the same project in NSW. It depends on the type of property and location.

Also, you shouldn't assess replacement costs on your own. Contact reputable contractors or developers well-versed in your market and property type to obtain reliable figures.

This will help you make crucial decisions, such as when to buy property when the price drops below the replacement cost, and build property when the replacement cost is lower than the price. This makes the replacement cost the perfect way to assess opportunities to create value.

Hence, the most significant advantage of using the replacement cost is that it lets you buy under intrinsic value. This provides you with capital gain almost instantly. You can negotiate an affordable deal, pay a reasonable price, and obtain tremendous capital growth.

You should also use this method to identify houses with less competition. These properties usually need some work to deliver high profits, such as cosmetic renovations. They might be derelict, putting many investors off buying them.

But this also opens an excellent opportunity for you. As fewer people are interested in places that require renovations, you enjoy less competition. Just make sure you can afford to revamp the house and maximise its potential.

Buying dwellings under their replacement cost is great, but where do you find these properties? The general rule of thumb is that you should avoid relatively new areas. For example, finding an undervalued property is hard in a housing estate built two months ago. It's only recently hit the market, making it tricky to calculate potential value.

Why? Because these properties have scarce historical data. They've only been around for a limited time, preventing you from making an informed decision.

This means you should focus on established properties. They hold their value better than new builds and usually outperform them long-term. They also offer higher capital appreciation without dropping too low in sluggish markets.

Another thing I want you to remember regarding the replacement cost is that it's not the same as the market costs allocated for improvements. Take a look at nearly any valuation report in Australia, and you'll see that the two figures are different.

As indicated earlier, replacement costs are driven by various other costs, such as building, labour, and government fees. The amounts vary based on the availability of materials and location.

The replacement cost can influence market values, but it's not the main driver. That role belongs to supply and demand.

If demand is lower than supply, market values are below replacement costs. In this setting, market values are generally unaffected by replacement costs, and the effect is amplified if supply keeps rising.

Many properties in remote areas are impacted by this trend. This allows you to purchase them for a lower price than the cost of building the place from scratch. The reason is simple – supply and demand give you the necessary negotiating power.

If supply and demand are similar, replacement costs and market values are more synchronised. Since there's strength on the demand side, the market brings about a rise in supply. As a result, more properties spring up because the cost of buying an established house is similar to the price of building a new one. This reinforces supply, as numerous developers decide to construct a place. These markets have a healthy volume, and you can normally fund them in regional centres or outer suburban areas of capital cities.

Another market condition you need to consider is when supply is lower than demand, leading to rising prices. This happens when some locations have high demand, but there's no way for supply to meet it. Many places are prone to this trend, like newly constructed inner-city areas or high-end neighbourhoods.

In rare cases, market values and replacement costs can remain at similar levels when demand eclipses supply. For example, the supply in Australian mining towns is sometimes reduced due to a lack of labour and trades, which leads to low replacement costs. The construction industry can raise the costs to even things out. However, this doesn't always work since the market may impose hefty premiums.

The last point about replacement costs you should keep in mind is that you need to mitigate the so-called replacement risk. This risk holds that your property can become economically or functionally obsolete due to new places coming into the market with similar rent. The economy in markets with higher rents may lean toward new properties to accommodate demand, making older options less desirable.

The first key to mitigating this risk is to recognise it in your transaction. If you're buying a house in a market with limited supply and growing rents, it's safe to assume that new buildings will jeopardise your position. So, you should consider switching to a different location.

The second key is to draw up plans to keep your tenants from abandoning your property. Cosmetic renovations are a great way to do so.

What Incentivises Sellers to Sell Quickly

The concept of buying properties under value might sound too good to be true. Acquiring one can be a massive boon to your portfolio and help you move on to your next house faster.

But why would anyone sell their dwelling for a price lower than the market value? After all, it's probably their most expensive asset. Why would people let go of it so lightly?

There are several reasons:

Death

One of the most common reasons people sell their house for a price lower than market value is due to the death of a family member. For instance, many deceased individuals will that the profits from selling their property be divided among family members. In these cases, the relatives may decide to sell the place under the market value to speed up the process.

Divorce

Divorce is another driver of undervalued properties. When two people are separating, the price of the house is rarely a priority. They usually want to sell the abode quickly, split the profits, and move on with their lives.

Defaults

When you think about the property market, you assume that sellers don't rush to seal the deal. They're aware of the value of their asset and don't mind waiting an extra week or two to find a buyer willing to pay the price. But that's not how it always works.

In reality, many sellers encounter financial duress due to defaults. They have trouble paying their mortgage after losing their job, or the bank has raised the interest rate significantly. Therefore, they can't afford to repay the loan, allowing the bank to foreclose the place.

Once the financial institution is in control, the story changes completely. The owners don't look to make a profitable investment with their repossessed property. Their motive is simple – minimising the loss and selling the property to the first customer who offers a fair price. Savvy investors are on the hunt for these opportunities, as they're conducive to hefty profits.

Other types of financial duress can lead to undervaluation, too. The owner may have suffered a crippling loss trading stocks or racked up enormous credit card debt. They need fast cash to solve their predicament, which is why they settle for a bargain price. It enables them to alleviate their problem sooner.

Seller Ignorance

Again, first-time investors generally assume that sellers are informed about the value of their house, but this is a far-fetched belief. The reason is simple – unlike stock market prices, property prices aren't listed. Instead, they're approximate and vary drastically.

Thus, some owners may be oblivious to the advantages of their property and fail to charge a high price. If you can find these sellers, you might be able to buy a stunning house for a bargain.

Subpar Performance

Subpar market performance is another factor that can make the vendor let go of their property for a lower price. If it's been on sale for a while or there haven't been any good offers, the owner may consider selling it under market value.

In most cases, poor market performance is attributed to inappropriate pricing. And the leading cause of inappropriate pricing is improper comparison. Keep in mind that the right way to compare properties is to consider places of the same general design and in the same condition. If the vendor bases their comparison on better-looking dwellings, their evaluation is probably off.

The time a property spends advertised for sale also depends on the condition of the market. In hot markets, a vendor typically receives excellent offers immediately. Conversely, vendors in sluggish markets are more likely to receive low offers. Some don't like to wait very long, so they sell the place under value.

Failure to Disclose Major Problems

Owners of deteriorated properties can't get away with concealing major problems. You can uncover everything during your inspection. Afterwards, the owner has three options – fix the problem, agree to a lower price, or offer you a credit to finance the repairs.

Vendors who fail to address the issues risk eliminating a large number of purchasers looking for a turnkey house.

Not Preparing for Sales

Sellers who don't stage and clean their place can also put off many potential buyers. They may not be able to afford a professional cleaning service, but this doesn't justify not addressing minor issues. For example, a dripping faucet or broken doorknob looks bad in the eyes of investors. They may suspect that the owner is hiding larger issues, allowing them to negotiate a lower price.

Hence, you want to pay attention to every single detail when purchasing a house. The owner is well-familiar with the house, but they may not be aware of all the trouble spots. If it's cluttered, smelly, or the walls are dirty, you might be able to buy it below market value.

Selling Agent Issues

Owners often hire agents to sell their houses on their behalf. However, trouble begins when the representative is out to move their property without involving inspections and marketing. Their only goal is to earn their commission, so they don't have the seller's best interest in mind. As a result, selling at a lower price is the fastest way to accomplish their goal.

On top of that, the agent might be unfamiliar with the market. It might be outside their usual territory, or they've just entered the area. They don't understand the environment and may underestimate the property.

Additionally, the sales agent may be superficial. They may only compare their recent sales to determine the property's value. They don't take the competition into account, leading to undervaluation.

Tenant Problems

Selling a house with tenants can be challenging, especially if they're difficult. For instance, they may only allow potential buyers to check out the place for a limited time. This discourages investors, resulting in less competition and lower prices.

Lack of Insurance

Sellers want to be insured to safeguard against several scenarios. A potential buyer may have an accident in the house and suffer injuries, enabling them to sue the owner for damages. This can also speed up the sale and make the owner settle for a low price.

Familiarising Yourself With an Area

The best investors have made millions by investing in undervalued properties. You can be incredibly successful, too. But first, you'll need to learn how to identify these dwellings. Here are a few pointers:

Leverage Data

Knowing the market is paramount to finding undervalued properties. The only way to understand it is to use data.

When considering your purchases, make sure to look at the price of other houses in the area. Go through past sales and see what dwellings are currently advertised for. By examining the average price, you can determine what to expect in the future.

Besides the price, you should also obtain many other essential details:

- What is the capital growth of nearby properties?
- Does the vendor offer any discounts?
- How long are local properties listed for sale?
- What is the weekly rent and rental yield?

The answers to these questions let you make an informed decision. You'll be able to target suitable properties more easily.

Uncover the Seller's Motivation

We've already established the reasons people sell their properties for lower prices. Your job is to figure out if any of them apply to your vendor and capitalise on them.

Direct conversations with the owner might be the best way to uncover their motivation, but you shouldn't have trouble obtaining the information from agents, either. You can discover several details that can help you turn the negotiations in your favour. Sellers motivated by relationship breakdowns, divorces, or financial issues, are normally keen on selling their house as fast as possible.

Although this doesn't mean you should take advantage of others, it reveals critical information – whether you can buy the place under value or not. If so, this tactic also lets you stay calm, as you know you're in the driver's seat.

That said, be careful while uncovering the vendor's motivation. Be sure not to disclose too much about yourself because the sales agent can use it against you.

Look for Hidden Gems

Another way to maximise your capital gain through undervalued properties is to apply the age-old investment saying – buy the worst house on the best street. Visit attractive neighbourhoods and look for a place that needs a little work. If it doesn't look good, the selling point is hampered. Therefore, do whatever it takes to make it presentable, such as embellishing the garden or installing new cabinetry.

The key to making the most of this strategy is to factor in all the costs beforehand. Oftentimes, investors overspend on the renovations and exceed their budgets. This keeps them from profiting, even if they've bought the house under value.

Avoid this situation by calculating your numbers appropriately.

Target New Infrastructure

I've explained previously that properties with nearby new infrastructure are conducive to high capital growth. But some of them can also be undervalued. Shopping centres, parklands, train lines, and other amenities help raise capital growth and rental yield.

However, don't go for just any property. Look for areas scheduled for development. These suburbs usually have many undervalued places whose worth will soar once the new projects are completed.

Additionally, focus on lighter industrial areas scheduled for rezoning. These can be a terrific opportunity to purchase undervalued dwellings. If you've done your research correctly and ensured you can pay for any shortfalls, you should rake in massive equity rapidly.

Still, be careful when choosing your property because newly gentrified zones can be tricky to value. If a house is unique and has massive architectural significance, comparing it to other places will be hard, if not impossible. There's minimal comparable evidence, and the market value might be subjective.

Go Through Older Listings

If you've already found a particular development, check out the properties already advertised for sale. Most vendors have a specific time frame to sell the property. As the limit draws near, they might be more willing to lower the price. It's customary for owners to ask their agents to drop the price if no one seems interested after two or three months.

Don't forget that you should also examine rental listings. Sometimes, landlords of places that have been vacant for quite a while may be ready to let go of the property for less money. This could be a remarkable investment opportunity.

Keep Up With Auctions

Properties listed for auctions can help you score a significant profit, mainly if the agent overestimates a house. Nobody shows up at an auction if the agent's starting price is too much. The property will thus stay on the market for much longer. Once it receives this label, getting the price tag down will be much easier.

But the reverse can happen at the auction itself. A property might be too expensive for all participants, but the owner may want to get rid of it immediately. Hence, the price can go down during the auction, allowing you to invest in an undervalued dwelling.

Buy New Developments After Completion

Purchasing off-the-plan properties (before the construction is over) is an excellent investment tactic. It lets you net great profits without attracting holding costs. Still, this doesn't mean you can't score bargains after the work is done.

In fact, this tactic can deliver even better results, but you'll need to choose suitable properties. Look for places advertised for sale 3-10 years after construction.

Many people think they'll make a lot of money selling in the post-construction period, but the market sometimes doesn't move in their favour. If the interest is minimal, they will lower the price to attract more buyers. Therefore, the place becomes undervalued. This creates the perfect opportunity for you to employ value-added strategies to acquire property and ramp up your portfolio.

CHAPTER 9

Property Financing Fundamentals

While selecting the right strategy to supercharge your portfolio is challenging enough on its own, you now have to think about financing your upcoming purchase, build, or renovation.

See, regardless of your chosen investment strategy, you still have to put in a significant investment to close a real estate deal. It's equally important to navigate the financing aspect of real estate investing.

The first step would be to unlearn one of the biggest misconceptions in property investing: that only people with high income or a lot of savings can become successful investors. Remember: the reality is far more nuanced than that.

Even on a low income or deposit, you can start building your portfolio. Likewise, you don't need to have a huge amount of cash lying around to fund your builds and renovations.

There are other financing options available to you, the most common of which would be securing capital from outside sources. However, taking out a real estate investment loan is easier said than done.

Real estate financing comes with terms you need to fully understand before entering into a contract. There are a lot of factors to consider before obtaining property investment financing, including your choice of lender.

In this chapter, we'll take a deep dive into the process of securing funds for your planned deals.

Know Your Options for Potential Lenders

There are three common ways to secure outside financing for your next investment deal. Each of these options have pros and cons you need to weigh up before deciding which way to go:

Mainstream Lending

Mainstream lending is the collective term used for taking out a loan from one of the major banks like ANZ, Commonwealth, NAB, or CBA. It is also referred to as a mortgage loan.

As I touched upon earlier, these big banks typically require a rigorous application process before offering you a property investment loan. After all, investment property loans are generally viewed as higher risk than owner occupier home loans for personal residence use. This is because investors can immediately walk away from a property that they did not buy as their personal residence the moment something goes wrong.

In a mortgage loan, the property itself serves as collateral for the loan. However, if you already have an existing home or property, you may be able to leverage the equity on that property to take out a loan from a mainstream lender.

Private Lending

Private lending is simply taking out a loan with a bigger investor looking to make an interest on their money. If you personally know one such investor, you may negotiate with them directly. Otherwise, you can speak to a broker who can connect you with their network of high-net-worth investors who may be interested in funding your next project.

This is a very common capital-raising strategy in property investing as private investors tend to require less rigid requirements than banks. However, the downside is that private lenders are not bound by interest rate caps that other financial institutions may have.

Joint Venture Partners

A joint venture is characterised by two or more parties entering an agreement to share the costs and returns of property acquisition, development, and sale.

This is an option commonly taken by investors who have enough working capital to purchase a property but not to develop it by themselves. They will then team up with other investors who would agree to take a stake in the investment deal by sharing all the costs, risks, and rewards that may be incurred from the deal.

Splitting the risks of investment deals is one of the most obvious advantages of entering a joint venture. However, having to deal with co-investors can be a risk in and of itself. After all, it may be challenging to agree on an exit strategy with too many vested interests in one property deal. This challenge is often what brings investors to favour private lending.

Now, let's dive into some specifics to fully understand how mortgages and equity come into play in the mainstream financing of your real estate investments.

Know How Mortgages Work

A mortgage agreement allows you to obtain properties without paying its full price upfront.

Typically, lenders will only agree to finance a chunk of the total purchase price, so you still need to come up with the down payment, which is usually 20% of the total contract price. Some lenders would allow a smaller deposit of 10%, but not without a caveat. In these cases, you would have to pay for lenders mortgage insurance (LMI) and possibly a higher interest rate.

After you put up the deposit or downpayment, the lender will then finance the rest, with your agreement to pay the loan plus interest over a specified number of years. If, for whatever reason, you fail to pay for the mortgage, the lender can take over the property in a process called foreclosure.

Your repayment rate would depend on a number of factors, the most important of which would be the bank rates set by the Reserve Bank, as well as the tenor of your loan. You can always use a mortgage calculator to come up with an approximation of how much your mortgage will cost.

A typical mortgage in Australia is set up for 30 years, and you may choose between two types of mortgage: variable and fixed rate.

Variable Rate Mortgages

Variable rate mortgages, interchangeably called variable interest mortgages, come with a fluid interest rate that could go up or down… depending on the interest rate officially set by the Reserve Bank of Australia.

At the time of writing, Reserve Bank Rates are at historic lows, so you may take this as an opportunity to take out a loan and make higher monthly repayments than the minimum set by your lender. This way, you can chip away at the principal of your loan, allowing you to manage your spending should interest rates increase in the future.

The tradeoff with a variable rate mortgage is the risk that your repayments will go up should the Reserve Bank Rate increase in the future. So, one of your biggest considerations when taking out this kind of loan is whether or not you'd still be able to make your repayments in case the future financial climate calls for higher rates.

Fixed Rate Mortgages

Unlike a variable interest mortgage where your monthly repayments may go up or down any time… a fixed rate mortgage entitles you to a fixed interest rate for a certain period of time, typically between one and five years.

This provides you, the borrower, with a level of certainty that even if the Reserve Bank Rates do go up in the next couple of years, you'd still be beholden to the same repayment amounts… at least for the term where your interest rate is fixed.

Of course, the downside is easy to see. Should interest rates go down in the next couple of years, you won't be able to benefit from lower repayments for as long as your current rate is still locked in.

Typically, fixed-interest mortgages also have more stringent rules. For instance, you might not be allowed to make extra repayments to shorten the length of the loan. Furthermore, should you decide to break your fixed-rate mortgage contract with your lender, you will need to pay a break fee, which is usually very expensive.

As mentioned earlier, you would need to put up a cash deposit, regardless of the type of mortgage you opt to get. So, what are your options if you don't have access to cash to cover the necessary deposit?

Well, you can always use the equity built up in your existing home in lieu of a cash deposit.

Understanding Equity

Equity refers to the value of your ownership in your existing home. Mathematically speaking, it is the difference between your home's market value… and what remains of your home loan balance.

For instance, if the market value of your home is $450,000, and you still owe $150,000 in your home loan, your equity would be $300,000. So, over time, as you pay off more of your loan and the value of your property increases, your equity also goes higher. An important point to make is that you can't actually use all your equity to buy another property. Typically, you can only leverage up to 80% of the equity you have in your home to fund another purchase.

Now, if the equity you have in your current home is enough to cover the deposit you need for your planned property investment deal, then you no longer have to put up a cash deposit. Of course, you would still need to deal with stamp duty and other legal fees, but having equity saves you the trouble of scrimping and saving thousands of dollars for your investment deposit.

Note, however, that borrowing against equity means you'll be using your primary place of residence as security. Having equity in your home is also not a guarantee that you can borrow against it, as everything still depends on your chosen lender's loan process and borrowing criteria.

So, what can you do if you're amenable to the aforementioned risks, but the current equity in your home is still not enough to cover the cash deposit needed for your planned investment? Well, there are a number of ways you can grow your equity, but note that each of these strategies require a long-term plan, so you might have to adjust your investment horizons if you're hoping to cash in on your home's equity:

Make Extra Repayments

Since equity is the difference between your home's market value and the remaining balance on your home loan… you can grow your equity by reducing your payable home loan.

Lump sum payments are not just beneficial for increasing your equity. They can also cut your future interest charges, as they would naturally help you gain full ownership of your current home faster.

Shorten Your Loan Term

Another way to increase your equity would be to shorten your loan term from the typical 30-year mortgage. Like the first strategy, this would require you to make higher repayments, but with the tradeoff of faster full ownership of your home and the ability to take out a bigger home equity loan on it.

Increase the Value of Your Home

The formula for calculating your equity is composed of two parts: your remaining loan balance and the current market value of your property. So, apart from chipping away at your loan balance, you may also increase your equity by adding value to your home.

To increase the worth of your home, you may add some valuable renovations, improvements, and maintenance works on it. Just make sure you have a clear picture of how much more value you can add to your home through these means, so you can increase your equity as planned and needed for investing.

Again, these strategies can work if you are not planning to invest in the near future. However, if you can't wait to start building your portfolio and the equity you can leverage in your home is not enough to cover the down payment, then you might not have a lot of options outside of coming up with the deposit.

Positive vs. Negative Gearing

Another huge consideration in financing your property investment is choosing between positive- and negative-gearing. Let's take a look at what each of these strategies mean and what pros and cons you can expect from both options.

Positive-Gearing

Positively-geared properties give you a positive cash flow from the moment you rent out your acquired property.

Here, the rental income you expect to get from your tenants is higher than the amount you pay to own the property. Since the rent outweighs your ongoing costs, positively-geared properties earn you an annual profit.

Let's say the cost of owning the property you want to acquire is $400 per week. If you are in a position to charge tenants $450 a week in rent, then your return on investment would be $50 per week or $2,600 annually. That's money going straight to your account.

However, the drawbacks of positive-gearing are much more difficult to spot than the advantage of putting cold cash in your pocket and increasing your borrowing power from the get-go. For one, you'll get taxed on your rental income, which in turn helps you leverage more from banks for future purchases. Positively-geared properties are likewise typically situated in regional or outer suburbs of capital cities especially when we are looking to buy houses with decent land size.

Negative-Gearing

The alternative to positively-geared properties is negatively-geared properties.

This happens when the cost of owning your property investment is higher than the rental income it will produce. The strategy here is to wait for the property to increase in value, so you can sell it for profit later on. However, it demands that you wear the costs of owning the investment property in the meantime.

There is no doubt that negative-gearing tends to put you in a tighter cash flow. This means you'd need to feed your property with additional cash for the entire time you're waiting for the value of your investment to grow. This likewise affects your borrowing power for future investments.

However, negative-gearing allows you to claim most of your losses—including depreciation—against your tax dues. Overall, it effectively reduces your taxable income. Furthermore, waiting on a good location with strong fundamentals almost always puts you in a position to gain far more than what you have to absorb in losses.

Choosing between positively-geared and negatively-geared properties has been the cause for a never-ending debate among investors. In the end, however, only you can assess your current priorities and cash flow situation in order to choose which strategy will work best for you.

At any rate, it pays to consult financial advisors and mortgage experts to come up with a plan that puts you on a solid investment path.

Crunch Your Numbers

After you've chosen your gearing strategy and shortlisted possible lenders to fund your next investment, it's time to crunch your numbers and find out how much borrowing power you have… before actually applying for a loan.

Knowing how much you can borrow is critical for your investment journey, as it helps you understand just how much you can spend on acquiring, building, or renovating a property.

Some of the factors that will come into play when it's time for lenders to calculate how much you can borrow include the following:

- Your current income
- Your expenses
- Any existing loans or credit you have taken out
- Your preferred loan term

These are general considerations. Note that different lenders would have different qualifications and criteria to come up with the amount they would be willing to lend you. This is why it's important to shop around since various banks will have different calculations of your borrowing power. The difference in your capacity as far as two different lenders are concerned might make all the difference between building your property portfolio the way you want it… and settling for investments you're not totally sold on.

Learn to Negotiate Loans

Savvy investors don't just have strong borrowing power. They also have a solid negotiating power which can get the loan terms and interest rates they want. To build a strong property investment portfolio that will allow you to quit your job or escape the toxic business that has enslaved rather than liberated you, you need to build your negotiating power to live the life you truly want.

Here are some ways you can do that:

Make Pricing Requests

At the end of the day, banks are not in competition with you. They are in competition with other banks, so if you can learn to play your chosen bank off with their main competitors, you may be able to put in a request for the price you want.

If you're currently with a major bank, ask them to beat the rates being offered by other major banks. If, on the other hand, you're working with a smaller lender, ask them to match the prevailing market rates. You can ask a mortgage broker to do this for you via a pricing request. Banks know that mortgage brokers can take your business to other lenders, so they are more likely to offer your broker the best rate right away if they want you to do business with them.

Consider Fixed Rate Loans

If banks are currently offering low rates, you may be able to maximise said rate by taking out a fixed rate loan. We have previously discussed at length the pros and cons of doing this, so weigh your options carefully. If investment loan rates are at record lows, you might want to consider taking banks up on that—at least your repayments for the next few years will be relatively easier for you to manage.

Refinance Your Loan

Some investors fall into the trap of thinking that their negotiating power goes down once they've signed a deal with one bank. However, you always have the option to refinance your loan if another lender offers better rates, provided you're not in a fixed rate loan where a break cost may apply.

The strategy here is to make it clear to your bank that you're willing to refinance your loan should you find better terms elsewhere. Note that banks will only offer you the lowest possible discount on financing if they know that you're prepared to take your business to another lender.

Let them know that you're not keen on just getting the loan process over with and will refinance when necessary. This will boost your negotiating power as banks would do anyting to make you stay.

Financing your property investments can be a long, arduous process. However, it's one that you just can't avoid as you start to build your portfolio. You just have to know how to play to your strengths and do your research to come out with the best possible terms that will allow you to maximise the projected gains from your investments.

CHAPTER 10

Investment Structures

Ever wondered what it would feel like to build wealth and create a stable future for you and your family through property investing?

While this question has been answered in different ways, I came up with a way to simplify them for you.

You see, there are multiple ways to own and invest in property in Australia. And the process can become filled with problems if you don't have a full understanding of the legal and financial frameworks involved in property ownership.

Once you've made the decision to buy one or more real estate assets, you should think carefully about the appropriate investment structure to use. This refers to the type or system of legal ownership for your investments.

It's a good idea to familiarise yourself with the available investment structures so you can minimise risks and avoid any legal and tax issues down the line.

For example, many people buy assets in their individual or combined names. But they didn't know that other forms of ownership would be ideal for their situation.

Now, the ownership structure you choose will depend on many factors. These include your budget, risk appetite, and the specific financial goals you set for the investment property.

Plus, it also helps to factor in the total costs of acquiring property assets in Australia. This is because what you'll pay goes beyond just the deposit and a mortgage.

Similarly, there are advantages and disadvantages to each type of property ownership structure. So, it is a must for property investors like you to consider the types of real estate ownership structures available.

In this chapter, I will be discussing the five different types of property ownership structures. These include ownership through self-managed super funds, companies, and trusts. I have also incorporated some examples to help guide you in making sense of the five different types.

Now, it's important to take note that just as there isn't a single "best type of real estate to invest in," each investment structure has its own advantages and disadvantages.

It's part of your role as a property investor to conduct your own due diligence to identify which structure best suits your goals and preferences.

At the end of the day, your tax requirements, estate planning, succession plans, and asset protection may all be significantly influenced by the type of property ownership you select.

And as I have mentioned, your property investment journey is personal.

This means the strategies that may work for one person may not necessarily have the same effect for you. There is no "one size fits all" approach. The same goes for the type of investment structure you choose.

Another thing to consider is that the ideas I will discuss in this chapter are from my perspective as a property investor.

If you are interested to learn more about the legal and tax frameworks involved for each structure, it's always best to consult your lawyer or licensed accountant before taking any action.

Factors to Consider Before Choosing an Investment Structure

As we go through each type of ownership structure, there are a few things you need to consider before making your decision.

Your final choice will come down to your financial circumstances, risk appetite, and your property portfolio's objectives. Ultimately, it all depends on which structure best fits your own circumstances.

- **Tax Efficiency**

This can be defined as being able to pay the least amount of taxes required by law. And tax efficiency is one of the most important factors in deciding your ownership structure.

Why?

This is because it will allow you to maximise the opportunities by legally reducing your tax liabilities.

Think of it this way:

If you want to manage your investment property and reap the best results, your ownership structure should be one that won't put a burden on how much you pay in taxes.

A financial investment decision is considered tax-efficient when it generates a lower tax outcome than another structure.

To structure your investment, you will need to have knowledge of the existing tax-related laws that are applicable in your circumstance. Of course, this doesn't mean reading through all the pages of documents and guidelines set by the ATO.

Getting counsel from a good tax consultant works just as well. They will give you the necessary information and help you get clear on your property and investment taxes.

- **Asset Protection**

Asset protection refers to the preservation of your personal assets from being used to meet a business creditor's claim.

What does this mean?

Let's say you have bad debt and other liabilities that you haven't settled. Without asset protection, you risk having your creditors acquire your property to make up for their losses or in case you default.

So, you have to create an asset protection plan to ensure your property is as far away as possible from other liabilities.

Some investment structures have different guidelines or approaches when it comes to asset protection. So, it is advisable to seek expert legal and financial advice when structuring your investment portfolio or when you are devising an asset protection plan.

- **Simplicity or Complexity**

The simplicity or complexity of an investment structure has to do with how much financial risk is involved. It requires an assessment of the risk appetite or risk tolerance you have, which is the measure of how much an investor is willing to incur in terms of losses within their portfolio.

But how do you evaluate how much your risk appetite or tolerance is?

The simple answer is that you should take into account age, investment goals, income, and comfort level in the overall investment.

This is a process that usually involves the help of a financial adviser. With their expertise, they'll match the volatility or price risk of the investments with your personal assessment.

Of course, the process of determining risk appetite or tolerance more often than not focuses on the tolerance for losses.

Undergoing a risk appetite and risk tolerance assessment will allow you to determine the target asset allocation for your portfolio and decide on the sub-allocation within a particular asset.

This will also help you to review and rebalance your portfolio on a regular basis.

What Investment Structures Are Available for You?

There are several options when it comes to structuring your property investment. Let's take a closer look at each one:

1. Buying Under a Discretionary Trust

Trust pertains to the relationship between a trustee and the beneficiary.

The trustee then has an obligation to hold the property of the beneficiary. This means the trustee will have legal ownership of the property as indicated in the trust deed. The beneficiaries, on the other hand, will hold the beneficial interest resulting from any income generated by the property.

A discretionary trust or family trust pertains to a situation where a fixed interest or entitlement in trust funds is not held by the beneficiaries.

The trustee has the choice to determine which of the beneficiaries will receive the income and capital of the trust, as well as the amount that each beneficiary would get.

But it must be noted that the trustee does not have complete discretion. This is because the terms of the trust deed stipulate that the trustee must distribute the funds to a nominated class of beneficiaries.

This means there are specific people who are privy to the stakes involved in the investment. So, while the trustee may own the property, everyone who is part of the trust may stand to benefit from the investment returns in one form or another.

Despite these drawbacks, discretionary trusts remain the most popular choice for ownership structures among investors. The reason is that they provide strong asset protection and distribution flexibility.

A trust can offer flexibility in succession planning as well.

If you directly own the property, it will need to be sold or given to your heirs after your passing. But if the assets are maintained in a trust, the trustee you appointed may continue to handle them as per your instructions.

Trusts, however, are not applicable for negative gearing concessions. This is when an asset does not generate enough income to pay its cost. When you are negatively geared, then choosing a discretionary trust as your investment structure may make your asset less tax-effective.

Keep in mind that trusts are complex legal contracts. And there are many things to think about before creating one.

Because of this, it's crucial that you seek expert guidance before establishing a trust for your investment property.

2. Buying Under a Company

As an ownership structure, buying under a company or corporation has several benefits. Some of them include reduced personal liability, tax breaks, and asset protection.

The great thing property investors find about this arrangement is that the property income is only subject to a 30% tax rate. For investors in higher tax brackets, this can result in significant savings during tax season.

This investment structure also protects assets from personal liability. Still, it should be noted that this aspect does not cover corporate liability.

Companies and corporations are not entitled to the same capital gains tax breaks as individual owners. Just like with SMSF ownership, there are several compliance requirements and legal obligations that you must be aware of.

This means that there is a higher possibility of you having to pay the necessary legal fees to maintain the investment structure.

Most of the time, buying an investment property under a company is used for business structuring. Since a company is a legal entity on its own, it possesses the same rights as a person. Thus, it can incur liabilities such as debts and can sue and be sued.

The company's owners have the power to limit their personal liability. So, they will not be liable for any debts taken on by the company name.

Your goal then as an investor is to become the main or sole shareholder of a company to enjoy the benefits of this structure.

Another option you can consider within this investment structure is establishing a company of your own for investment purposes. This is generally the most beneficial and common practice among self-employed high-income earners.

Note that this option would require more capital from you compared to buying shares from a company. As the main or sole shareholder of the newly established company, you can then effectively make decisions for the company.

It must be noted, however, that companies cannot be created for the sole purpose of avoiding taxes.

What's more, this investment option is also accompanied by risks. While your percentage share of ownership determines the amount of returns you receive, it also represents the losses you will incur in the event that the property doesn't make any profits.

This means that the main or sole shareholder risks incurring most of the financial losses from their investment in the company.

Now, it's also good to take note that not all banks are open to lending money to company structures. Typically, this happens when their system is unable to handle business loans or because their credit team lacks the necessary training to evaluate business loan applications.

On the other hand, several banks have excessive demands, such as requesting tax returns for a newly formed company. Other banks also don't offer professional discounts for loans named to a company.

When you do manage to take out a loan in a company's name, that company will be both the borrower and the owner of the investment property. And all of its directors will be obliged to guarantee the debt.

3. Buying Under a Fixed Unit Trust

A fixed unit trust is a trust where the rights of the beneficiaries (unit holders) to income and capital are fixed.

What does this mean?

It means that they are not subject to any discretions on the part of a trustee. And the asset will be unitised in a way that the rights are divided amongst the beneficiaries. The division will then depend on how many units they have been issued individually.

Unlike a beneficiary of a discretionary trust where there is no proprietary interest in the property, a unit holder in a unit trust may have a proprietary interest in that property. This is generally part of a relevant proportion of all unit trusts, depending on the terms of the trust deed.

And similar to buying under a company, it is possible for a unit trust to have different types of units with different rights attached.

Fixed unit trusts are generally more attractive for investors due to the fact that net income and capital gains are delivered to unitholders before taxes.

To put it another way, the unit trust is tax-exempt. Instead, each unit holder is subject to taxation for distributions received from the trust at their individual marginal tax rate in accordance with the Income Tax Assessment Act.

It must be noted, however, that it will be a "non-fixed trust" for the purposes of the trust loss rules if the trust deed allows for other methods of valuing new units or the redemption of units, even if it is a unit trust with no discretionary elements.

Such a trust will need to satisfy more tests than a fixed trust if it is to carry forward its losses.

4. Buying Under an SMSF

A Self-Managed Superannuation Fund (SMSF) is a superannuation trust structure where the members are also the trustees. This allows them to have more control over superannuation investment decisions.

It gives the members the opportunity to borrow money to purchase investment properties within the SMSF while, at the same time, giving them the authority to run it for their benefit.

As trustees, the SMSF members have the responsibility to comply with the super and tax laws.

The corresponding responsibilities include the need to annually appoint and pay for an auditor to audit your fund. You will also need to keep records for at least five years and in some instances for as long as 10 years of your SPSF-related expenses.

What's more, you will be required to annually valuate your assets and complete your annual return. Trustee meetings must also be held to discuss any decision the fund makes, especially around investments. Moreover, you need to make a detailed investment strategy and regularly review it.

Any changes in your financial circumstances such as when you lose your job will not terminate your liability in the SMSF.

This is because of SMSF's highly regulated and complex ownership structures. It places strict limitations on what improvements you can make to the properties in the SMSF.

It is very common among lenders to require the beneficiaries of the SMSF to personally guarantee the loans. This is because borrowing through an SMSF limits the bank's lost funds recovery ability to SMSF-related assets in case of a default.

Given the complex process involved in investing in an SMSF, it is advisable to make the necessary preparations in advance. This includes doing your research on different investment strategies, setting a personalised investment plan, and getting an audit from an approved SMSF auditor.

Choosing the Right Investment Structure

Throughout this chapter, we talked about what investment structure is all about and its purpose. We discussed how an investment structure can pertain to how your investments are legally owned. Similarly, investment structure can be considered just as important as the investment itself.

Things to be considered include the financial circumstances, risk appetite, and your property portfolio's objectives. By understanding and weighing the pros and cons of the aforementioned variables, you can determine the appropriate investment structure that best suits you.

Choosing which investment structure depends entirely on your own personal circumstances. What works for one person may not work for you. So, it's best that you consider all possible options and assess how well each option can benefit you.

Being aware of the benefits and drawbacks of each structure, as well as what your borrowing capacity is, will give you an edge in maximising your profits and in effectively managing your property portfolio.

In relation to this, I discussed the importance of knowing the different factors that must be considered before choosing an investment structure, namely, tax efficiency, asset protection, and simplicity/complexity.

Tax efficiency is being able to pay the least amount of taxes required by law, while asset protection is the preservation of your personal assets from being used to meet a business creditor's claim.

On the other hand, the simplicity or complexity of structures is the assessment of the risk appetite or risk tolerance you have and your preference for the investment method and structure.

The great thing about investment structures is that you have many options available to you. So, you may even come up with a few alternatives for how to structure your property investment, depending on your long-term goals and financial preferences.

While it may be simpler and less expensive for married couples to take out loans together, there may be tax advantages to taking out loans in one partner's name or the other.

On the other hand, a company or trust structure can be the best option for those looking to reduce their obligation and safeguard their stake in other assets.

The best strategy is to consider all possible options and assess how well they can benefit you.

After all, the best investment structure is one that presents you with the best long-term tax outcome, and allows you to maximise the opportunity for strong future returns through your property investment.

Now, I completely understand if you might have certain fears about choosing the "wrong" investment structure. For one thing, it's difficult to change your structure once you have already made your investment. And it can reduce your overall return of investment.

But here's what you should always keep in mind:

You will be able to minimise risk by being knowledgeable.

Study the benefits and drawbacks of each structure before making any decisions. And don't be shy to consult your accountant, mortgage broker, and lawyer for guidance.

Only then will you be able to consider the best fitting investment structure for you.

CHAPTER 11

The Property Investor Mindset

Property investing can be a powerful wealth generator. Abhiram and Pavitra, Tom and Crystal, and Anju and Lokesh know this. Every single one of our clients understands this to be true. I've *seen* it come true for myself and the myriad of clients I've helped across the years.

The property investing framework I've shared with you over the last nine chapters is the exact same framework that has resulted in great results for me, my clients and mentees.

We sought undervalued properties... negotiated the best terms for real estate investment loans... and added value to those acquisitions using any one or a combination of the four value-add strategies I discussed with you: the granny flat, cosmetic renovations, buying established houses or land for subdivisions, and going for new builds.

Now, it's time for you to walk the path paved for you by those who have gone down the property investment path before... keeping in mind the four key elements of building a successful property portfolio:

1. **Property Education**

Your first priority right now should be equipping yourself with all the education you can get about properties and real estate investment.

This is the single most important investment you've got to make right now because property education will not just put you in the right mindset for investing, it will also show you all the various options available in the market... what you can take from these options... and which one is best suited to your own needs and risk appetite.

2. **Build a Team**

I've emphasised this over and over again in this book, but it's worth repeating that before you start investing, you've got to have a good team. You need a good mortgage broker, a solicitor, an investor savvy accountant, and perhaps even a property buyer agent on your corner.

One good tip I can leave you is to seek people who are not just good consultants… but are property lovers themselves. You don't want to put yourself at risk by using the wrong person in your team. If you can find experts who have built an impressive portfolio of their own, then all the better.

3. Take Action

All the education in the world and even the best team on your side can't generate any wealth for you… unless you take action. Implement the strategies I've shared with you in this book, and start building your portfolio as soon as possible.

In the last chapter, we discussed positively-geared and negatively-geared properties. While both strategies have merits, my personal take in that neverending debate leans in favour of positively-geared properties.

Why?

Because it's the strategy that will allow you to take more action. After all, the fourth key element in building a successful property portfolio is this:

4. Rinse and repeat

Your goal is to keep on buying more properties so you can achieve your goals sooner rather than later. This will only be possible if you stick to positively-geared and capital growth properties that can give you more capital for further investments.

But when I talk about the element of rinsing and repeating, I am not just referring to buying more and more properties. I'm talking about repeating the entire four-step process outlined right here. So start from investing in more education so you can expand what you know…

Then, continue building your team as your portfolio grows…

Finally, acquire more properties with your expanded knowledge and refined team to get the highest possible return on your investments.

I know that no part of this real estate investing journey seems easy. However, it's equally true that no part of the journey is impossible.

Remember my story?

I started my property investing journey with zero knowledge. And yet, after three and a half years, I had a multi-million-dollar portfolio that helped me quit my 9-5 IT job.

And the one thing that kept me going when the going got tough?

It was my big WHY.

I've told you about my stint in corporate and how I realised it wasn't the life for me when I heard that my daughter cried the whole time my wife and I left her at daycare. I didn't want to continue living a life where I couldn't spend time raising my daughter and being present for my wife.

I also disliked the fact that my parents saw less and less of me as they grew old, since I couldn't take time off from my job.

I wanted my time back, and that was my big WHY.

Now, you might be thinking about starting your real estate journey because you want a Ferarri, or the latest iPhone every time a new one drops. But trust me when I say that you need a bigger 'why' than these material things.

Because no one really needs a Ferrari. No one really needs a new iPhone every year. And no one really needs a hundred holiday flights a year. And when the property investing life becomes a bit too challenging for your liking, you would think you can just walk away—because you have no compelling reason to continue struggling.

But if you have a bigger why…

Whether that be to quit a soul-sucking job and get your life back…

To have more time to spend with your growing family…

Or to provide your loved ones with a better life…

You will always find a reason to keep going.

After all, you will soon realise that property investment is more than just finding the right tricks and strategies. It's also about psychology and how you can bring the right mindset to investing.

And now that I've taught you pretty much everything you need to know about the strategies that will make you a successful investor… let me leave you with a few principles that will help you build the property investor mindset:

Apart from having a big why, you also need to…

Have a Long-Term Vision

Property investing is far from being a get-rich-quick scheme. It's a great way to achieve financial security, but the road getting there might be longer and more winding than you would like it to be.

It's a long game with many highs and lows that can span decades of your life. And if you don't have your eye on the long-term goal, you can easily get distracted by every shiny thing you encounter along the way.

Accept That There Will Be Risks

While it's true that property is one of the safest investment vehicles you can explore, it is not without its fair share of risks. That's a reality you need to accept so you can be smart enough to only take the risks you can calculate and manage.

After all, if you do your due diligence in educating yourself about which properties are best suited for your needs and goals… you need not be exposed to grave risks.

Anticipate Market Fluctuations

One of the biggest mistakes you can make as a budding property investor is to panic at the first sign of a market dip. The market will fluctuate. That's a fact. Australia's housing market has gone through countless price cycles… but history will tell you the ups have far outweighed the downs. This is why seasoned investors do not sell all their properties at dips.

The key here is to understand that the market may rise and fall, but over time, it also grows and stablises. So, don't panic and ride it out.

Block Out Noise From the Media

I've touched upon this earlier, but absorbing too much noise from the media can throw you off your game. There is a lot of speculative, incorrect, and unsubstantiated information out there, but nothing can get you a more accurate reading of the market's pulse than studying the market yourself—and consulting property finance experts.

Following property news is fine… as long as you can sift through the noise and take only what you need to know.

Keep Emotions Out of It

The only time your emotions should play a big role in your investing journey is when you're looking for your big 'why.' After that, you should always remind yourself that you're not investing in these properties to live in them.

As such, every deal you negotiate, close, renovate, build, or sell is but a business transaction to you. That's why it pays not to let your personal emotions override sound business decisions. A great example of this would be not going over-the-top with renovations you personally like, so as not to price your property too high that it might become too difficult to sell.

Remember that the best investors can be optimistic and ambitious while remaining calm and rational.

Once you have your big 'why' sorted out and you've mastered all five principles of having the right property mindset…

All that's left to do is to take action and start your property investing journey.

There's no reason for you not to be able to replicate—or surpass, even—the great results that I have helped many other people achieve in this journey.

So, don't let your fear of the worst that could happen hinder you from living the life you want. Having a strong property portfolio can be your passport to better things in life… as it would earn you the financial freedom you need to start living the life you've always wanted.

Don't settle for less. Start investing and be right on track to live a life of no regrets.

CHAPTER 12

The Importance of Setting Goals and Knowing Your WHY

Some years ago, I was working as a software engineer back in India and my career seemed to be going on the right path. So much so that in 2007, my company sent me to Melbourne on a work-related assignment.

What I thought would be only a six-month assignment turned into a more than two-year stay.

During that time, I grew to appreciate the opportunities offered in Australia. I was earning money in dollars, which helped me to fulfill a lot of my childhood dreams like buying a car and building my savings.

So, I moved to the country permanently once I was offered a local job in 2009. That same year, my wife and I decided to get married. We then moved to Sydney and started a new chapter in our lives.

I stayed in that nine-to-five job for some time. While I was making a decent amount of money through it, I soon found myself becoming time-poor.

At some point, I began having no time for my wife and later with my daughter who was born in 2015 – my work took up every single second of my life. And when I had to drop my little daughter off at daycare, which happened every day, she constantly cried... And that broke me. Even though my daughter felt sad, I couldn't do anything but bring her to daycare and go to work. That frustration brought me to tears as well.

For a lot of people, leaving their children at daycare was perfectly normal. But for me, it didn't sit right at the time. Especially since I wasn't spending enough time with her already.

I realised that, yes, I was making steady progress in my career and my income was decent. But I no longer had time for the people I cared about the most.

That made me desire to find a way to spend more time with my wife and daughter while maintaining a positive cash flow that would provide us with the lifestyle we wanted.

In addition, my parents were encouraging me to stay in Australia, but they wouldn't be able to live here. My parents and I were extremely close, so that fact was devastating. The most we could do was go and visit once a year. And that would cost us a pretty penny.

Not only did I have little to no time to spend with my wife and daughter, but I also had to be away from my parents for a long time.

I reached the point where I really needed things to change.

My purpose was my family. To be able to spend time with them, to be close to them, and to be able to support them financially and emotionally. I also wanted a future where I could play with my daughter, go on dates with my wife, and bond with my parents.

And to make it happen, I needed to break free from the shackles of working for money and let my money start working for me.

That's what I did.

Now that I had a vision, I took the first steps to make it come to life. And the avenue I chose was property investing.

I was already exposed to property investing in 2010 when I attended a seminar about passive income. Even though I was interested, I lacked the drive to actually do anything.

This time was different. So much so that I quit my job and became a full-time property investor. And I haven't looked back since.

That's how my property investing journey started. I found an extremely important WHY that led me to take action. A profound reason that was connected to my heart – not superficial, like wanting a Ferrari or a BMW.

As a result, I went from having zero knowledge of investing to having a multi-million dollar portfolio and more than a million dollars in equity in just three and half years. I boosted my confidence, self image and helped change my perspective about money, time, wealth and belief that all this is possible for me as well.

My point is that having a clear goal and direction in mind is vital to becoming a property investor. Without it, you won't have the drive to consistently apply yourself to investing.

Your goal will keep you going.

Yes, there will be challenges along the way. But when that happens, looking back at your goal will push you forward. When you look at the potential future, you'll see that the obstacle you're facing is just another small hurdle to get to that.

My purpose enabled me to get to where I am now. When you find yours, you will be able to reach greater heights as well.

This chapter is all about finding your WHY and learning how to set your property goals. This way, you can create a clear path that will lead you to financial freedom and success.

Why You Need to Set Property Investment Goals

I have a question for you:

Would you rather be ten years older and have a multi-million-dollar property portfolio, or be 10 years older and stay exactly the same as you are?

Chances are, you will choose the first option. After all, everyone wants to be rich. But here's the reality I want you to remember:

It's incredibly difficult to become successful if you don't have the proper mindset.

I need to reiterate this idea because having the right mindset is the foundation of how you will achieve success in the property market. Part of this is becoming goal-oriented so you will have the proper road map for doing things.

You need to pick a goal that's extremely personal to you, something that you're really yearning for. It could be anything – planning for retirement, buying a house to live in, wanting to give your children a good future, or buying rental property for passive income, for example.

If you don't have any clear goal, you'll just be wandering aimlessly in the world of property investing. You won't be able to achieve anything, and you'll just waste valuable time and effort.

At the same time, setting an arbitrary goal like becoming rich will just lead you to failure. That's because you don't really know what that represents. It's hard to visualise such a broad goal.

By setting a specific goal, you move one step closer to it because you now know what to do.

So, think long and hard about what your goal is. Do some serious introspection for a few days, weeks, or even months – there's no need to rush. See where you're at now and where you want to be. Identify the things that you're happy and unhappy with.

Remember, it should be a goal that's connected to your heart, and something that will always keep you motivated. For me, it was my family. But for you, it could be anything else that you deeply care about.

Once you figure out what your goal is, you can plot that on the map, and draw the lines from your starting point to your destination. This way, you'll know the concrete steps you should take to achieve your dreams.

You'll also get to determine the risk factor and effects of each decision much more easily if you have a specific objective to achieve. By being strategic, you'll identify which actions will have a positive and negative impact on your goal.

You can also create a realistic timetable as a result. You'll be able to analyse what your assets are currently, your ability to acquire property, how lucrative real estate is in your area, and how much potential profit you can make. This will enable you to take action in a timely manner.

If you want to have twenty rental properties, for example, you can gauge how many properties you can acquire each year, and take appropriate action.

You'll also have reasonable expectations and won't feel down when you don't achieve your goal immediately. There's also going to be a reasonable standard for success and failure.

Overall, having a clear goal will give you the proper motivation and information to make well-strategised actions and decisions in property investing. It'll also keep you from burning out since you have a future to visualise. You'll also get to maintain reasonable expectations.

How to Set Your Goals

Now that you know WHY to set your goals, it's time to learn HOW to set them.

When selecting your goals, you shouldn't do it without any rhyme or reason. It needs to be done systematically while considering as many factors as possible.

It must also be specific and detailed and outline the entirety of your vision and the actions you need to take to reach that vision. Also, it should be as straightforward as possible to avoid confusion and keep you focused.

While you can take time to set your goals by yourself through trial and error, and slowly figuring out how to do it, that's going to take up too much valuable time.

Instead, I'm going to teach you a systematic method to set your goals and achieve them without feeling overwhelmed.

Identify Your WHY

Obviously, the first thing you need to do is to identify WHY you want to become a property investor. This will be your primary, overarching goal that will drive you to move forward.

As stated earlier, this must be a deep and profound reason that is connected to you and the people you care about. It can branch out to something materialistic, but it should still serve that main goal.

Simply put, your WHY will be your primary motivator and what you will remember when facing challenges, difficulties, and obstacles.

By identifying this reason, you can start taking the first steps to take action. Think of your WHY as the foundation of your building that'll determine how to build the walls, ceilings, and everything else.

Do not undervalue the significance of this action. The property you acquire, how you finance them, and every other decision you make will be influenced by your purpose.

You may already understand your WHY and only need to take a moment to write it down. It's also possible that you decided to invest in real estate without fully considering the reasons why.

In any case, establish that goal before continuing.

Do Your Research on the Property Market

After identifying your primary goal, it's time to research and expand your knowledge base.

Most likely, you're starting with absolutely zero experience. And if you push through with property investing without research, that's a recipe for disaster.

It's essential to learn first instead of immediately diving into investing so you can protect your resources and make informed decisions.

Fortunately, there are a ton of free and paid resources available to you to learn more about property investing. You can read ebooks, watch videos, listen to podcasts, sign up for online courses and many more.

Aside from general property market information, you should also research how your local real estate operates. Check which areas are being developed that could increase in value and what areas are potentially stagnant or decreasing in value.

If you don't take the time to learn, you'll likely buy into bad deals. You might also fall into the trap of buying high and selling low. Or worse, you might miss out on perfect deals since you don't know how to spot them.

Make sure to research local laws and consult with financial specialists if you need help to acquire funding to buy your initial property. They'll assess your financial capabilities and help you choose how to start investing.

And if you want to become a landlord, there are certain things to consider such as rent, maintenance, tenants, leases, and more. You need to make sure that you can afford that property now and into the future.

Keep in mind that it's especially dangerous to get into owning rental property without proper research. Mistakes can cost you your money and land you in legal trouble if you're not careful.

List Down Your SMART Goals

A common mistake that people, property investors included, make that prevents them from achieving their goals is making them too broad and vague.

Your goals should be SPECIFIC, MEASURABLE, ATTAINABLE, REALISTIC, and TIMEBOUND. This is to make it easier for you to formulate steps to achieve it.

Instead of saying, "I want to own rental property..." say, "I want to own a dual-income for rent, earning me $6,000 a month by December 31st, 2023."

The second statement is much better since it's exact. Knowing that you want to own a dual income property lets you know how much money to save. With that, you can budget your money accordingly.

The problem with nebulous goals such as the first one is it's difficult to approach. There are too many lingering questions that need to be answered.

Being unclear can also cause information overload and prevent us from doing anything. It's also much harder to plan for a general goal since you won't have clear steps to do it.

Having super-clear goals allows you to take appropriate action by removing all the guesswork. It forces you to consider all factors and create realistic targets.

When setting SMART goals, you need to consider your finances, the time frame, and the exact nature of what you want. It'll ensure you're not wasting time on an impossible dream.

Break Your Big Goals into Smaller Goals

When all of your goals are excellently written and incorporate the SMART principles, you can now break them down into simpler goals. Think of it like creating a cascading list to achieve that initial goal, with the goal that can't be broken down further at the bottom.

Create a checklist starting with the most uncomplicated goal, and keep going up until you reach the objective you began with. By doing this, you can figure out all of the steps that you need to take. You can also plan ahead and use your time wisely by scheduling what task to do per day.

Checklists also have a powerful psychological effect. When you check off a task, it gives you a powerful surge of dopamine. You feel a sense of accomplishment that replenishes your drive and helps you move forward.

It also makes a complex goal much more digestible and easier to handle. You won't be overloaded by an immense task if you break them down into blocks that are easier to do.

There is genuine strength in simplicity when it comes to property investing. With so many choices and alternatives available, it's easy to become distracted, overanalyse things, and lose focus.

Breaking down your goals and creating checklists out of them will help you avoid all that.

Set a Timeline

Coinciding with having a checklist for each goal, you should have an overall timeline for your property investing journey. Having a timeline sets a final goal post that will help you plan properly.

So, identify long-term and short-term goals and how you plan to achieve them. For how long do you plan to keep a particular property? Will it be for two, five, ten, twenty, or thirty years?

Doing this will help you assess the risk-reward ratio of each property and the benefits of holding for a short or long time.

Also, discuss equity expectations with your bank or financial advisor over a meal. Consider how long it will take to reach these equity targets, mainly if your long-term goal is to amass a sizable property portfolio.

Here's a tip: the first property is always the most difficult since it requires a lot of effort and preparation. But once you have your first property, the second, third, and fourth should be more straightforward.

This is a common trait among investors. So, even if you can't forecast the future of the real estate market, you can establish specific objectives and timelines and alter them as you go along.

Turn Your Actions into Habits

Every time you force yourself to do anything, you're using up your limited supply of willpower. And eventually, it will just run out.

To avoid the need for more willpower, you must convert your goals into habits. The actions you take to achieve your goals should become so ingrained that it feels like brushing your teeth or taking a bath.

These actions should take no effort at all and should be entirely natural for you.

At first, it may seem complicated. But it gets easier as long as you do it consistently. The more you repeat these tasks, the more it becomes second nature to you.

So, make things like checking real estate prices, finding new listings, and maintaining your properties, become part of your daily routine.

By doing these every day, you get to constantly look for new opportunities and streamline these processes to make them more effective and efficient. You also get better at these actions daily, which can snowball into better results over time.

It's by turning these actions into habits that you can save a lot of brain space for more important things. You could use it to take time on important decisions, learn more skills, or even form connections with other property investors.

Looking into Your Future Property Investment Journey

In summary, goal-setting is a crucial part of your journey as a property investor. It's what will keep you on track and motivated and enables you to complete your objectives.

When you have a purpose when investing in property, you can actually stay committed and create financial change in your life.

Additionally, your goals should be systematic and methodical and account for every factor and variable. It must also make your life easier and improve your skills and capabilities as an investor.

Setting goals is also vital so you can create proper schedules and use your time wisely. And it'll also let you break down goals into manageable chunks that can be done one at a time.

When you have a clear goal in mind, you open yourself up to so many possibilities. Nothing is clouding your thoughts, so there's less friction between your mind and actions.

It's possible to own a series of units that give you a substantial amount of passive income every month. It's possible to buy a run-down house in a good neighbourhood for cheap, then fix it up and sell it for a massive profit. It's even possible to own a multi-million dollar high-rise skyscraper in an ultra-expensive city like New York or Las Vegas.

All you need to do to make those things happen is set a goal and continuously and meticulously work hard to achieve that. Consistency is the key to success, after all. As long as you follow these principles, these goals are an achievable reality.

Keep in mind that achieving your goal takes a lot of time and effort. So, I want you to start applying these principles to your life right now.

Start a property investment goal that you can achieve by the end of the year. It could be saving up enough money for the initial down payment on a house, setting up a property for rent, or even just learning more about property and real estate.

By applying what you learned in this chapter, you can begin your journey to becoming a successful property investor.

The first steps you take matter the most, as that's what will start your momentum. Even if it's a simple step, that action can serve as the catalyst for your future success.